Becoming
The Shero

Dr. Anissa Short
Visionary and Coordinator

DEDICATION

---·◦❀◦·---

Shero is defined as a woman admired for her courage, outstanding achievements, or noble qualities. This book is dedicated to the women that have made and continue to make a positive impact on our lives and the lives of many others. We salute and pay great respect to the following. They are our sheroes.

J. Meralyn Conard
Priscilla Edwards
Gracie Green
Laverne Harper
Katie Hobbs Hines
Peggy Housch
Virginia Kemp Arvella
Vasser Lewis
Angie Lyle
Lillie Lee McLean
Bertha L. McGee
Charlene Renee McQueen
Rosa Rand
Martha Lee Henderson
Remizer Cooper-Seals
Lee Ella Smith
Dr. Kaye Smith
Willie Mae Sykes
Vicky Tate
Berniece Lewis Tunstall
Jurline Utley-Walker
Hortense A. Watson
Josephine Watson
Betty Lou West
Dimple White
Irene Lily Williams

ACKNOWLEDGEMENT

As with any collaborative undertaking, it takes the gifts and talents of many to bring a project to fruition. This project is no different and because of that, it is only appropriate to extend gratitude to the many that served to assist us, the "Becoming the Shero" team.

Thank you to Speakerazzi for being the first to help in giving voice to this project. Your commitment to hearing from us all and allowing us a platform from which to share was greatly appreciated. Thank you for the flare and energy you added to each engagement.

To the team at Your Anointed Designs, thank you. From the first introduction until the completion of the final project, you were a joy to work with. Your vision and talent are a gift.

To Dr. Norma Mclauchlin, we extend our heartfelt gratitude. Your role as a mentor and advisor to the coordinator of this project is immeasurable. May all that you pour into the lives of everyone come back one hundred-fold? To everyone that served as our cheerleaders, supporting us along the way, we say thank you as well. You were the wind beneath our wings.

Table of Contents

FOREWORD

———◦◦∞◦◦———

The process of becoming a Shero is infinite. There is not a destination attached to her evolution; only a journey that can be measured by her strength, ability, and willingness to want more for herself and those who are around her.

We often view a Shero as the female version of a female hero — but her depth exceeds what we see on the surface. The heroic traits of a woman are embedded in her DNA - to be strong, resilient, and endearing is not an afterthought; but built-in characteristics that define her survival. The life of a Shero oftentimes goes unnoticed. We do the seemingly impossible — balancing career, family, education, relationships, faith, and peace.

The world only sees the results of her labor but never the process of progress.

A Shero goes beyond the typical roles that society says are appropriate for women. A Shero knows no bounds to her dreams and refuses to have a scarcity mentality. A scarcity mindset dictates a life "without" because of the fear that we are not worthy or good enough. Having a scarcity mindset puts a glass ceiling over our potential. Sometimes the worst-case scenario is not trying versus trying and failing. We must believe that we are abundant and everything we are meant to have, we will have. Everything we are meant to lose is for good reason.

And every piece of adversity that stares us in the face is only for a season. We must believe that our potential is limitless and refuse to think that it is anything less. Saying that something is not going to happen because of past experiences or sabotaging what "could be" comes from the self-belief that we do not deserve it. We do. We deserve anything our mind allows us to dream about. Just give permission to take action on the pavement.

Sometimes others will not see who we are or who we have the potential to be. It is called a vision for a reason. Sometimes we are called to do things that others cannot see because of their own limited perceptions. Do it anyway! If we can see, hear, smell, touch, and taste it, it is ours. Confirmation does not always need to come from the validation of others.

You cannot promise that today's version of yourself will always be applicable to tomorrow's challenges. Life will always present situations that will call in to question what you think you know to reveal what reality really looks like. When reality sets in, it forces you to adjust.

Pivoting is an essential trait of a Shero because she knows that life can change in an instant. But the beauty of her attitude shows that she will never change who she is amid adversity, but she will show up ready to tackle what is in front of her. As you continue to read through these pages, you will find the heart of a Shero in every story. Each individual author has poured their wins, losses, and lessons into a literary work that is meant to inspire you and charge you to take action in your life. They all may wear many hats — wife, entrepreneur, sister, friend, community advocate, ministry leader — but their tenacity always shines through. A Shero is truly multidimensional and a force to be reckoned with.

When I was asked to be a part of this project, I immediately wanted to be involved. As a business owner and host of Pink Lemonade Podcast, I was eager to meet the women of the anthology. During the month of May 2020, I talked to the authors and learned their back stories. Each person brought a lesson that blessed my life and I hope that their experience helps you find the freedom and courage you need to be the Shero you desire to be.

~ Whitney L. Barkley, M.S.
Host of Pink Lemonade Podcast

INTRODUCTION

Like many young children on a Saturday morning or weekday evenings, I would watch shows that depicted superheroes. Most of the time, the characters were always male and included a story line that would result in them saving the day, whether a damsel in distress or some major threat to the city.

Every young boy in my family or friend at school would want to be one or the other. This, in turn, would mean that the rest of us (the girls) would be forced to witness their amateur attempts to reenact an episode, or if we were lucky, we could be the damsel needing them to come to our rescue. A tablecloth or large bath towel would become their cape. Leaping from the sofa, monkey bars or tree in the yard would be their interpretation of leaping from tall buildings. We would use the power of our imagination to see the web they would shoot across the room. And, although I sometimes participated, I was never amused. None of what excited them excited me. That all changed; hmindsowever, when I was introduced to Diana Prince.

Diana Prince, the assistant to Major Steve Trevor by day, was a superhero like none other. She was the consummate professional during her day job, but when duty called, she would transform. A quick spin and she would reveal herself to the masses wearing gold bracelets that could stop bullets. She could read minds, and her lasso, when used, would bring the truth out of anyone. Her method of transportation was a jet, and she was the pilot. And no matter what the assignment, whether flying to her destination or subduing culprits, her hair and makeup were always in place. This superhero had the *"strength of Hercules, the wisdom of Athena, the speed of Mercury and the beauty of Aphrodite"* and while this description suggests that she was a goddess like none other, I grew up to believe and understand otherwise. As a child, I thought that this superhero, or Shero, was disguising herself by day as Diana. As an adult, I now know that Diana was the Shero, and that the superpower that she possessed is evident in many of the women that I knew and would come to know.

When it comes to strength, women possess what it takes to give birth to nations and at the same time lay the foundation of what is needed for that child to grow into whatever they desire to become. That same strength can be seen in the tears they cry during heartache and in the way they shake off the hurt to move through the day. This strength is evident each time they come to the rescue of their family or friends, and in the way they commit to one another effortlessly when it comes to a common cause. They are those who operate in purpose and are committed to the task set before them. They are change makers, the voices of truth, and the big thinkers. Even amid fear, or after a major disappointment or setback, and even when they know that someone, they love has messed up royally, they get suited up again. They are parents, educators, doctors, home makers, scientist, politicians, business owners, ministers, and civic leaders.

They are the women that we know, and love, and those who truly inspire us. They are the real superheroes, our everyday Sheroes.

When this assignment came to mind, there was no doubt in my mind or to the mind of the authors, when I shared with them the vision of this book that this platform would resonate with women of all ages. It was certain to each of us that each story, or each offering of transparency, would allow another to realize that while we may come from different backgrounds and upbringings, much of what we experience is the same. Ultimately, the overall objective was to affirm and inspire, to encourage and to empower. As you read the contributions of each author, reflect on the Sheroes in your life. In doing so, salute them because of their commitment, be empowered by their focus and drive, and be challenged each time you see them make the shifts and pivots needed to create a better life or world. In addition, realize that you are a Shero to someone too. Never doubt the impact you are making in the lives of others. Be that person willing to come to the rescue of others in need, and whether your day is easy or a challenge, be sure to represent with style and grace. There are others coming behind you that need to see your superpower. They are depending on you to be their Shero, too.

~ Dr. Anissa Conard Short

Becoming the Shero

The term "Shero" surfaced in the 1830s to honor women, regarded as heroes. Over 2 centuries later, it still describes women of all cultures and backgrounds who possess power. The power to stay true, the power to embrace pivots, the power to following their paths and the power to think beyond. "Becoming the Shero" highlights thought provoking testimonials from women of different races, backgrounds, and upbringings. And together, they are showing the world the beauty of becoming and remaining a Shero.

SHEROES ARE COMMITTED

—•◦❈◦•—

"Commitment means staying loyal to what you said you were going to do long after the mood you said it in has left you."

FIRST FRUITS
~Anita Blue~

What is the first thing you do with your paycheck? I know there are things in life considered to be a top priority. Mortgage or rent must be paid. Utilities and other fees must be satisfied for the month. The list goes on. I get it! But what is the FIRST source to which you give of your "first fruits?" My definition of first fruits is what you do with your money before you pay your monthly expenses.

Every fruit comes from a seed. Every seed is intentionally planted. Therefore, you must also be intentional when it comes to your money. As a business owner, I have heard many times how important it is to put money aside for yourself. Some coin this practice as "paying yourself first" and others refer to it as a "rainy day fund." I know people who have a certain amount of their paycheck automatically deposited into their savings account. All of these, in my opinion, are wise decisions.

I want to take it a step further. Consider that person in your life who encouraged you to start your own business. It might be a parent, a sibling, a spouse, a spiritual leader, or a mentor. Long before you received your first paycheck, that person planted a "seed" in your mind. Perhaps it was a seed of encouragement or a seed of confidence. Maybe it was a seed of knowledge, information, and wisdom. Regardless of the seed, have you ever considered going back and planting a portion of that seed – through your paycheck – into their lives?

Meditate for a moment on the things they said to you. "You can do anything you put your mind to." "I know it's hard, but you can't give up." "Let me know how I can help." "Here's some money to get you started." Now that you have some experience and a measure of success, have you thought about sowing a "thank you" seed back into those individuals? I am certain that they are happy to see you moving forward and emerging in your business. After all, they did affirm you – verbally, mentally, emotionally, and financially. Why not thank them monetarily?

As I ponder the idea of a "Shero," one thing I know is that she realizes she did not get to where she is solely on her own. Someone or something inspired her to step out on faith, take the risk, count the costs, and just jump in. Countless business owners, such as myself, were fortunate to have someone who was a springboard for our quantum leap. They said, wrote, or did something that ignited a fire of inspiration within. And it was that ignition that helped the Shero to look the unknown in the face and say, "I'm still going to give it a shot."

Every Shero can probably attest that the journey after taking that quantum leap was not easy. There were obstacles to overcome. There were fears to face and move past. There were situations where she felt she endured unfair treatment. There were times she fell flat on her face. Despite her good intentions and best efforts, she was misunderstood. But a Shero had something that those seemingly negative experiences could not take away from her. And that is those seeds of encouragement, inspiration, and exhortation that she received from others before she started her business journey. It was those words and deeds that gave her an inner fortitude, which was stronger than the outer failures. That is why she can get back up and try again. That is why she can regroup her thoughts, revise her plan, and regain a greater determination to move forward.

A Shero understands how important it is to sow back into the lives of others. She recognizes that those who gave her strength, and those who she could pull on when she needed it most deserved to be appreciated. She understands the importance of giving back to her community. I believe the beauty of giving back is you could receive something in return that perhaps money cannot buy. What do I mean? A Shero does not give for the sole purpose of that person giving back to her or to receive special recognition from the community. The purpose is to express one's gratitude toward the receiver. Giving is a way of acknowledging the significant role someone played in your life.

So, what should you expect to receive back? Your result of giving may be that your business increases. It could be you have another level of peace in your home and in your relationships. You may get an idea that will transform your life and the lives of others. What I am saying is that you may not get a monetary return from giving your first fruit, but you may receive something far greater in value; something that money cannot buy. When a farmer sows an apple seed, he does not reap a mere apple seed. Instead, he gets a harvest of apples. These apples can provide much more than what the seed alone could yield. Think of all the things you eat and drink that are made from apples: apple pie, applesauce, apple cobbler, apple jelly, and apple juice. What you enjoy from the apple is far greater than the simple seed. Yet that harvest of apples was inside the seed all along. Could it be that the harvest you see in your business today is a direct result of the seeds planted in you in the past?

When you set aside a specific amount from your paycheck to earmark it for that person(s) who sowed into you at the beginning stages of your business, this is known as the "First Fruit." When you gift someone monetarily because they inspired you to start your business, this is known as the "First Fruit." You would not be able to serve the number of customers and clients today if it had not been for the seeds planted in you by those who saw your potential.

Let us be the type of business professionals who give back to those valuable seed planters.

BARREN BRIDGES
~Monchaily Hendricks~

Remember when you first fell in love? You know that jaw-dropping, heart pounding moment that took your breath away. Where you realized, with certainty, exactly what you want. Well, that is what inspired my business. However, it was not just one love that drove me...it was two. I fell in love with a little boy and a spreadsheet. From these loves, an entrepreneur was born.

Love number one: a tummy ache turned into a baby. It was a deliciously sunny day in the quaint city of Brunswick, Maine. The trees outside my bedroom window were barely swaying and the sky was a beautiful matte shade of blue that really had me mesmerized. My hubby was at work and I had absolutely nothing to do. It was the perfect day but there was something wrong. A tummy ache. Yep, a tummy ache had plagued me for three days straight with no mercy and I could not take another moment of it. So, I went to see the doctor.

(Knock. Knock.) Hello, I am Doctor Johnson.

So, what brings you in today, she said?

(Sigh) Well, I have a bad stomachache that will not go away. All I need is some medicine, but Pepto Bismol is not working. Do you have anything stronger? I said.

She takes my vitals, asks all the routine questions, and says she wants to run some tests first. Honestly, I thought tests were overkill for a simple, stomach flu; but I did not care as long as I got medicine. Reluctantly I took the tests and headed home. As soon as I got in the house, I started gnawing on a plain slice of bread trying to soothe the nausea. I had not finished half of the slice when the phone rang.

Hello? Hi, this is Dr. Johnson. I have your test results. Congratulations! You are expecting. WHAT?!! Oh no! I do NOT have time for a baby. This is stomach flu! I am sorry this is not the news you wanted. However, we think you are at risk, so we need you to come back to the hospital to check for an ectopic pregnancy. Can you come now? Wait a minute! Not only is it NOT the stomach flu but there is something wrong? Ugh, fine. I will be there soon. (Click)

A zillion thoughts were swirling through my head. A baby, now? My husband is going on his first deployment in two weeks. This is NOT the time for a baby. I do not even have time to do the baby peas and carrots dinner. Plus, I must pick him up in 15 minutes from work. What am I supposed to say? I know! I will call mom.

(Ring) Hello? Hey mom. Okay, first stay calm! I need you to focus and answer one question. Okay, what is wrong?

I am pregnant and something is wrong, so I need to go to the hospital. I am picking up hubby in 15 minutes. How do I tell him?

AHHH! A piercing scream bursts through the phone.

Mom!! I told you to stay calm. Focus! Get excited later. How do I tell him we are having a baby in 15 minutes?

Tell him a knock, knock joke. A joke, mom? Seriously?

Yeah, make it fun.

Uhm, okay I will run with that. I will fill you in later. Thanks mom! (Click)

Quickly, I scribbled a joke inside a blank greeting card and hopped in the car. I pull up to the front of his squadron to pick him up. As he hops in the car, I hand him the card in the envelope. He smiles at me looking really puzzled.

Hey baby. What is up? He says.

Umm, I need you to read this card before we drive off, I said anxiously.

Umm, okay, he says.

He opens the card, and it reads: "Knock, knock. Who is there? Baby. Baby who? We're having a baby and I have to get to the hospital in 10 minutes." My adorable hubby then looks at me, smiles, makes a circular motion around his stomach and then points at me and says; "I'm so proud of you!" Proud of me? Umm, you helped. I certainly did not do this by myself. He just laughs and we drive to the hospital.

After arriving at the hospital, I am quickly rushed to the ultrasound room and some tests are taken. It was not until this exact moment that it really hit me. I am having a baby?! Ahh!!! And what is wrong with my baby? Why can't I have a normal pregnancy like the people on TV? As I wait for what seemed like forever, the doctors confirmed that I was in fact pregnant. I was 6 weeks pregnant to be exact and it was an ectopic pregnancy. This was a real shock for me. Not just that I was pregnant but the fact that prior to that point, I was told that I was barren. I was under the impression that I could not have children; so, a sudden pregnancy caught me off guard.

Now, at this point many moms would be freaking out over how the baby will survive and what damage would happen to them with this risk. However, my mind went to a completely different direction. I had no doubt that my baby would survive because I am a survivor of many things. I have survived sexual abuse, bullying, being drugged, raped and the list goes on. If I could survive all of that, then I know my baby will survive in my fallopian tube. What worried me the most was how he would face the world once he was born? How could I keep a child safe in a world full of violence, racism, impossible standards, and suffering? How could I be there for him anytime he needed me? How could I become his Shero? I was already in love with my child before he came out. I had no idea what to do but I was determined to find a way to protect him.

Honestly, I had no idea 'how' to become my son's Shero, but I did know that working away from home would hinder business, but I needed something to bridge the gap between my dream and my lack of experience. You know how God works things out in mysterious ways? Well, His mysterious method for me was a Mary Kay Consultant. Makeup was never my thing, so I had no idea why this sweet lady was talking to me at all. As an introvert, being outgoing is not something that comes to me naturally. So, when friends are made, it is usually because the other person is braver than me. However, this encounter was not about makeup. It was about a basement. Most beauty professionals speak about their products and how you should try them. This woman was different. She was not trying to sell anything to me. Instead, she was looking for help with her cluttered basement that she could not walk into. Her team was growing, and she needed to create a multipurpose space in her home. She knew what she wanted but did not know how to get it done. As she was expressing her concerns about how to do it, I volunteered. Organizing has always been a talent of mine so I jumped at the chance to help her.

A few days later my newborn and I went to her home, stroller, and all, to organize her basement. It was so...much...fun! Moving things around and transforming a space from chaotic to charismatic was a fun adventure. Love number two: a spreadsheet sparks joy. When I finished, she was so impressed that she asked me what else I was good at. I mentioned that I loved making excel spreadsheets, so she let me make one for her business. Building workbooks has always been an easy thing for me to do. The thrill of formulas and playing with cells to create a list is my idea of unwinding. It is just a fun toy on a computer to me. Yet, this spreadsheet was more than a creation to her, it sparked joy. Her amazement with how I can build and make it user friendly really inspired her. Next thing I know, she was telling every consultant on her team and everyone she met. I had clients coming out the ying yang! My little baby and I were rolling all over Maine doing business. A woman, a basement and a spreadsheet had become the bridge that brought my business to life. Every business journey is not sweatless. The bridge to my business dream was there but it was not a smooth walk. That bridge was fragile! The rails were made of rope and the floorboards were loose. Sometimes I walked on it and a plank would come out from under me. To truly cross this bridge my steps had to be cautious, patient and determined.

So, what am I saying? Not every step in business was a cake walk. My client group may have started strong but not every client loved my skill set. Some clients were not impressed and the ones that were, often wanted to shortchange me in price. There was much to learn as an entrepreneur. Basic things such as taxes, pricing and marketing were all new for me. No mentor was there to call and coach me into success. I had to encourage myself with the help of my husband who saw greatness in me. Did I always believe in my business? Nope. I tried to quit all the time; sometimes weekly. It was hard and I felt like a fish out of water. My relatives were not known for starting businesses and most thought I was doing too much trying to be with my son every day. Over the years I learned that businesses do not thrive on perfection, experience, an entourage, or even money. Businesses are built and maintained by love. There must be a constant foundation of love to keep you going even if you have no support. For me, my love was a little boy and a spreadsheet. The unconditional passion I had for my child fueled my business and helped me become the Shero he needed. The question is not 'should' I start a business. What you should ask is 'why not'? A Shero is not a fearless woman. She is a real woman who dares to cross any bridge to achieve a dream. I am that woman.

Will you become the next Shero?

USE WHAT YOU HAVE!!
~Peggy (Liz) Green~

My appetite for entrepreneurship started around the age of 13 or 14. I have always been a creative person who loved to read and sit outside under the sky. Sometimes I would fall asleep under the big tree by the road doing so. I remember summers of summer camps or staying home with smaller siblings, being I was the oldest girl. This summer, maybe '96 or '97, there came a popular string for crafting that children were into. They had different colors, and some would glow in the dark. It would come with instructions to make key chains, bracelets and even necklaces. I worked hard at building big ones as well. School started the following fall, and some students took notice of my string crafts. They got excited about them and decided they wanted certain colors. I began to sell the strings for a small fee, and I would give some away as well.

Being a student in middle school, I was also a part of an organization that introduced me to competition. I would always do my best to come out on top. I have awards for being top salesperson and placing Top 3 in an Essay Contest. It was very liberating to work hard at something and see the fruit "literally" of your labor, but also to help others win. It was during this time in my life that I learned that being a team player is important.

As I progressed with string-making, I gathered my nerves to ask my Mom to purchase bulk candy so I could sell it at school. We had a school store already filled with goodies, but children wanted the small candy. I had eight other siblings so I knew that we could always use extra cash as well. Week after week, we would make the 30-minute ride to the store where we purchased lollipops, Laffy Taffy, Now & Laters, etc. This was the best idea as my customers would purchase hundreds of dollars a week. In fact, I became known as the "Candy Lady" and as special requests would be extended, I did my best to supply them. This experience taught me that good customer service translated to good business. I was the Candy Lady for several years following.

My childhood was filled with misunderstandings. Domestic violence existed in our home for years causing severe instability. As children, we did not know what to expect during early morning preparations for school. Some days would go well, and then there were other days when our mornings were disturbed due to a raging man. Fights with my mother or mattresses thrown from the bed before sunlight, did not necessarily translate to missed time from school. And, since we did not know about domestic abuse shelters, we had nowhere to go. As hard as this experience was for us all, the resilience of my mom shined through. She did her best to provide for us and her hot meals were always something we could look forward to.

In 2003, my son Ja'Quaves was born. I was doing well for myself at that time; however, his entrance into my life shifted everything. I had to not only think about my future, but his future as well. I knew that if I wanted a better life for my son, I had to do more. This is when I decided to use what was in my hands! I reached back to the lessons taught to me from my mother. I had the know-how and skills to cook and bake, so I began baking cakes—caramel, caramel with pecans, pound cakes and jelly cakes. The extra money really came in handy to pay for daycare and the extra expenses of having a child. It was not always easy but with will and determination, we did well until I obtained a better paying full-time job.

When Ja'Quaves was a toddler, I was terminated from my job. My nerves were wrecked. I did not know what I was going to do to make ends meet to continue to take care of us. A year or so before this incident, I was offered to join a Direct Sales Company. I passed on the opportunity, but now that I was jobless and in need of income, I decided to give it a try. I was skeptical and intrigued at the same time, but soon realized that the flexibility of this opportunity worked well for me. My son could be with me when I was working, and soon my customer base began to grow as did my confidence. Those were critical moments for me as I was literally showing my 3-or-4-year-old how to be an entrepreneur. I was earning more money working for myself than I had ever earned working for another company. In that journey, I met some awesome people, began to travel, and see and meet others that inspired me to succeed at a higher level.

Several years later, I began to pray for guidance and understanding. I wanted to give birth to what grew inside of me. I began to explore herbs. I had suffered from asthma for years and found the need to work on other areas of my health. What I had begun to apply to my own life, I shared with others. The more herbs I used, the better I felt and this improved quality of life resulted in my pursuing another business opportunity. My stepping out on faith allowed me to show my son that moving into another direction is necessary if you want to improve or grow.

By way of my choices and experiences, my highs and lows, my son better understands that hard work with faith yields great results! I have shown him that just because you fail in one area of your life at one time or another that does not mean that you are not growing. Together, we have come to understand that when unexpected tests come, we can turn back to the familiar or re-evaluate, re-assess, re-set and re-start.

Even though my journey was not easy, it was the experience that showed me that life is not just about me. It started with me. Then it became about my son. Now my life's ambition is about creating generational wealth and leaving a legacy. I want my story of success to be the blessing that blesses others.

SHEROES THRIVE IN THEIR LANE

"Listen for the call of your destiny and when it comes, release your plans and follow."

~ Mollie Marti ~

ENTREPRENEURSHIP: IT'S IN MY DNA

~LaTondra C. Lewis~

According to the Epistle of James, he asked, "For what is your life. It is even a vapor that appeareth for a little time, and then vanished away." Psychology today says, "The actual meaning of life is to fulfill your purpose in life and accomplish your goals." To add to their definition, the meaning of life is that which we choose to give it. These statements cannot be argued.

To experience the quest for being, one should have purpose. Purpose is an act you do with determination, this act or aim becomes a design that has been created, fashioned, executed or contributed. The design then becomes a prototype, model, outline, map, or blueprint. As a result of a plan, intentionally purposefully and consciously dreams are created by design.

Conceived on the heel of the assassination of the late Reverend Dr. Martin Luther King Jr., my purposed filled amniotic journey began. Awaiting my arrival, my parents, both native Mississippians spoke blessings and equality over my future. My future would surpass the agony and hardships they encountered during the days of sharecropping, the Civil Rights Movement, and the Jim Crow Era. On May 17th, as the people of old would say, "in nineteen and

Sixty-Nine," my amniotic journey came to an end. I was welcomed by a young couple with love and compassion. The year 1969 was a year of purpose and adventure for America. Sesame Street debuts on the Public Broadcasting Service; Sly and the Family Stone ranked number 5 on the Billboard Hot 100 chart with "Everyday People;" the Edwin Hawkins Singers ranked 93 as well with "Oh Happy Day" and Apollo II was the first spaceflight that landed Commander Neil Armstrong on the moon. This year ended the decade of the sixties hope and progression for the African American community moving into the seventies.

My journey into entrepreneurship began with my parents the late Robert and Arvella Lewis. This young couple with goals and ambitions became small business owners in a little small Tennessee community. They were determined to succeed and help others along the way. A factory worker with a sixth-grade education and a beautician with a high school diploma, created a place of business for others. Many stylists earned a living by becoming self-employed at VEL's Beauty Shop. This business served the community for thirty-five years. VEL's was one of many African American businesses in the community. While the foundation had been laid, I could only imagine my parents' business concept was based on Habakkuk 2:2 "and the Lord answered, and said, write the vision, and make it plain upon tablets, that he may run that readeth it." Simply stated, a vision or thoughts written down, becomes solidified. The vision written helps us to organize one's planned path into entrepreneurship.

As an only child, I can remember going to work with my mother as young as three years old. Over few years, I was introduced to other black business owners that were a vital part of the community. Those businesses were thriving entities greatly supported by the community.

These introductions helped shape and mold my dreams and visions. Going back in time, I would pass time by sitting on the porch of the salon as a little girl, and observe the negative influences of street life unfold before my eyes. Amid the chaos of a debilitating life (for some), the community stood strong. This small nook of a community heralds camaraderie of churches, schools, civic leaders, and advocates. Those were the days of cohesive neighborly community engagements.

As a young teenager, going to work in the family business on Saturdays was non-negotiable. My mother would say, "You cannot make money sleeping in the bed, you have to go to the money." She then added, "You have to have money in order to make money." Shortly after her 1-minute lecture, my father would quote the Apostle Paul by saying, "He who does not work, neither shall he eat." Then I would gather myself for the day. Those Saturdays were full of "shop talks" and errands.

The late poet, Maya Angelou, quoted in several of her speeches, "people live in direct relations to the heroes and sheroes they have." For me, this statement is indicative of my family. Although my parents were business owners, they shared an entrepreneurship vision with my maternal aunts, uncles, and first cousins. They were noted stylists and barbers, and recognized salon owners in their perspective cities. They demonstrated and modeled their profession well. I guess it is true the apple does not fall far from the tree. Seemingly they all exemplified excellence by investing in the community, serving with humility, participating in continual education classes, and dressing impeccable for work. As a result of their success, I was privileged to have met many black owned manufacturers and distributors in the industry while attending major hair shows, conferences, marketing, and sales trainings.

To hail from such a great legacy of stylists and barbers has been an honor. This legacy has spanned over fifty plus years. Summer vacations did not stop me from working in the family business, no matter what city I was in.

Time moves forward a little more and the days of high school began. Cosmetology was available for study at my school, but I decided to stay on the academic track. Shortly after graduating, I entered college in hopes of pursuing a degree in biology and gross anatomy; I was intrigued with human growth and development. This major introduced me to a more in-depth approach to the life cycle. Taking these classes I learned how to embalm and conduct autopsies. I shared my little bit of knowledge with my mother as she went to the local funeral homes to style her deceased client's hair. Prior to graduating from undergrad and changing my major, I accepted my calling to preach the gospel, even though I ignored the call for ten years.

After graduating from college with a degree in social work, I fulfilled my promise to my mother and enrolled in beauty school. She was elated. My mother assisted financially through my journey in the industry. Sometimes she challenged me on theoretical application. Six months into beauty school my mother would become ill. May of 1997 to be exact, she was diagnosed with Ovarian Cancer. She did not allow the diagnosis to stop her from living. Six months later, November 1, 1997, she passed from the disease. The death of my mother was a hurtful experience. With the support of my dad and family I knew we were going to make it. I took on the task of eulogizing my mother's life at her Home going Celebration. Then life regained a sense of normalcy for me. I relocated the salon up the street from its original location.

Cosmetology class was going well and one year from my mother's burial I was diagnosed with breast cancer. Another journey through chemotherapy was not new to me. I had to end my cosmetology classes so that I could complete eight rounds of chemotherapy treatments and thirty-three counts of radiation. July 30, 1999 all treatments were over. As a young 29-year-old, I was ready for the world. During post chemo, I developed Lymphedema in my right arm. This disease is restrictive and limits your mobility if not properly treated. Life is back on track; the shop is thriving at its new location and things went well for the next two years.

Cancer knocks at my door again in 2002. I repeated traditional chemotherapy. This time four chemo treatments and thirty-three counts of radiation. This diagnosis moved my father to ask me to sell the Salon. He wanted me to heal without the stress. This was one of the hardest decisions I had to make, but I persevered through prayer and counseling. I regained normalcy again.

From my late twenties to my mid-forties, I experienced the death of two friends who were brutally murdered. I had two more surgeries, a hysterectomy, and breast surgery (ductal papilloma). On June 16, 2013, my father passed on Father's Day from Acute Myeloid Leukemia. I found myself eulogizing another parent, the last parent living. The start of my bloodline has ended. My circle of immediate family is no more. However, through all the challenges I kept pushing toward economic freedom and the opening of my own business.

For my 40th birthday, I made a promise to myself that I would be back in business by the age of fifty. My goal was to launch a small bed/breakfast. God saw differently and He gave me a Holistic vision. For years I assisted individuals to have a healthier lifestyle through food, nutrition, meditation, and exercise. My ministry encompassed the teachings of mind, body, and soul, coupled with one of my favorite scriptures 3 John 1:2 "Beloved I wish above all things that thou mayest prosper and be in health, even as they soul prospereth."

On August 1, 2019, I obtained my business license to the newly established Take a Pew Holistic Health Lounge. The launch did not occur until January 2020. Two months after opening Covid-19 makes its arrival. I had to strategically shift my sales from brick and mortar to delivery and curbside. Social media platforms became a prevalent marketing tool. Digital online sales were explored, and good old-fashioned retail was welcomed with social distancing and masks.

This process has taught me patience and perseverance through pandemonium and a more intense faith walk. I admonish anyone to follow their dream. Write your vision, build your foundation, and stand on the promises of God. Execute your plan and watch your unique business unfold. Psalm 125:1 Tells us "those who trust in the Lord are as mount Zion, which cannot be moved but abide forever." In other words, trust in Him, lean on Him, Him only and He will see you through.

Twinkie Clark penned these words, "Is my living in vain." Her sisters would echo back "No of course not!" Up the road is eternal gain. As much as I have lost over the years. I am going to keep pushing. My living is not in vain. Life for me is not a dream on a rowboat drifting down a stream. "Life is not a having and being, but a being and a becoming" (unknown). Create a legacy, follow your blueprints, and start walking in your purpose. I encourage you to write your vision. The late Shirley Chisholm once said, "You don't make progress standing on the sidelines gossiping, whimpering, and complaining. You make progress by becoming a part of a movement to introduce new ideas and other perspectives."

Keep pushing forward!

STAY CONNECTED
~JurLonna Walker Hermon, MBA~

Get ready to leap! The journey of building a business can be a roller coaster and a lonely road to travel. One minute you feel like you are on top of the world, working the vision you created. The next minute you are wondering if you made the right decision. Becoming a SHERO is a journey, not a destination. My own journey began when I was a child. Growing up, I can recall having my hair done at the salon. I was so fascinated as I watched the hairdressers create masterpieces upon my own and the crowns of other women's heads. There was no YouTube in those days, but I had my own version of the popular video platform just by being in the hair salon every other Saturday morning. It was so interesting to me. Around the age of 11, I started to care for my own hair. My first hairstyle experiment was a "Salt-N-Pepa" haircut. My mom was so upset. When she took me to the hairdresser she said, "Fix this child's hair, please!" The hairdresser examined my masterpiece and said, "There isn't much to fix. She actually did an amazing job." That was the beginning of my business journey. I was only in the sixth grade and I began to have people lined up in my parent's living room waiting to get their hair done. When I look back, I realize this was just a hobby that I enjoyed because I did not get paid for it.

However, I did have an entrepreneurial spirit. I was doing something I loved and using it to serve others.

Later in my life, I became tired of going to a job day after day without any purpose. This is when I got serious about starting my business. I set out on an adventure to find out what I was called by God to do. The work I was doing was very impactful and meaningful, but I still felt like I was meant to do more in my journey of life. After many self-assessments, I discovered that I am designed to help others discover and walk in their purpose. From that revelation, JurLonna Walker, LLC was formed. It consists of life coaching, speaking, training, and authorship. In 2017, I authored my first book, Follow Your Breadcrumbs, a guide that helps individuals to discover their purpose.

Throughout my entrepreneurial journey, I received an understanding of the type of life God wants me and others to live, and that is how Holistic Livin' Enterprises, Inc. was created. Holistic Livin' is a concept of Kingdom Living (KL) for all areas of life, which means living the best life that God created for you to have according to the word of God. Holistic Livin' Enterprises, Inc. delivers the KL message through wellness, travel, and lifestyle.

The businesses I have created are designed to impact several areas of influence within our global economy: business, religion, family, health, and media. My goal is to leave an imprint within each of these areas. JurLonna Walker, LLC brings resources such as books, teachings, and coaching to the global economy by incorporating the agenda of the Kingdom of God. Holistic Livin' Enterprises, Inc. introduces the concept of what it means to live a faith-based life to enhance one's quality of life. My struggles have not been about others, they have been about me.

WHEN YOU PRAY, GOD WILL ANSWER.

I prayed for God to reveal to me what I am supposed to do. I realized that he answers our prayers by opening doors of opportunity. When opportunities present themselves to us, sometimes we struggle acting on that opportunity. I believe we struggled moving forward because we water down the vision by looking at others who may be in the same arena, thinking I do not want to compete, I want to be different. Anything God gives you will be different from the next man or woman. It may appear similar but when you take what God gives you, he brings out your uniqueness towards that area.

My own struggle with acting on opportunity happened once I became a life coach. When I first started coaching, it was almost unheard of at the time. Now it is a flooded market. Everyone and their mother seemed to be a life coach, and I wanted to be different! Because the market was flooded, I had the mindset of quitting. I did not want to do something that everybody else was doing. Instead of trusting God with the vision he had given me for my life, I withdrew into fear and the familiar. What a terrible mindset to have! If everyone thought this way, there would only be one preacher, one doctor, one teacher, one chef, and the list goes on. The question that needs to be asked is how do I stand out in a flooded market? The answer to that question is to be authentic in your brand. Just Be You!

To become a SHERO I have learned that you must ask God to show you your blind spots in business. When you look at your business you see it through your own lenses. You must ask for guidance from God to see things the way he sees them. One day I asked God a series of questions. Why do I keep going in this cycle regarding business? Why am I not advancing in the business arena? Immediately, he shared with me the following:

- You assumed if it is God, then you do not have to work for it. That is far from the truth.

- If you do the natural, I will do the super.

- You must put in the work. Whatever is difficult for you, give it to me.

- Stop standing on the sidelines and go play. I have something waiting for you.

- You have not been showing up. If you show up, I will bless you. Nothing is too difficult for me.

- How are you going to let your light shine if you are locked up in the house?

- Nothing, I mean nothing, is too big for me.

- Be part of the community, let your light shine.

- Be disciplined! Trust me, trust your voice, I live inside you and you are in me. Stop second guessing yourself and work.

- Remember the difference between toiling and gathering. Once you are in place, I will send you the people you will; gather; that is your work.

- When it comes to partnerships do the same as you did when you were getting married. Ask me to show you their heart, their intentions, and motives.

- Stop judging a book by its cover. That is religion.

- You do not move forward in anything because you assume it is not me.

- You never know what I have planned for those situations. Do not assume. Ask me to reveal their intentions and motives.

With all these revelations, it is time to do something about them, right? Do any of these revelations speak to you?

NO WEAPON FORMED SHALL PROSPER

The death of a loved one, especially a parent, can have a serious impact on you. In 2016 my mother passed away. It felt like the umbilical cord detached from me all over again, but her death ignited a fire in me. One thing I realized more than ever is that I am determined to fulfill my purpose on earth, and I will not go to the grave full. I turned my devastation into fuel for my purpose in life. The lesson I learned from her passing is do not allow life circumstances to hinder you from completing the assignment you have on earth. My assignment is bigger than me, my family or friends. The assignment is like a baby to a certain degree. As a mother you will do everything in your power and will to protect, nurture, and care for your baby. The same thing applies to your assignment or purpose. It must be protected. Life circumstances can destroy you and your purpose if you allow it. It is okay to mourn for a moment, but you must move on with joy!

The way I overcome challenges of self-defeat and death are to stay connected to my source of power. As you can see above, when I have an issue, I run to my Creator to get the remedy. I also recite scriptures of promises with the faith that they may come to pass. Between these two strategies, they help me to move forward and do so in joy. I realized long ago that I did not want to go to church just to go; I wanted to use it as a training ground for success. That meant I had to believe God's word for my own life rather than reading the bible as a good story. I am a big believer that you must find your tribe.

There are many good churches that serve many parts of the body of Christ. I am associated with a church that teaches Faith in the marketplace. That is my tribe and training camp. It is good to listen to a variety of speakers, but the one who truly has a voice in my life is the one who is in my tribe. See my spiritual father (church/tribe leader) has words and wisdom for where I am going. An awesome speaker can motivate and inspire me, but they are not the ultimate voice in my life. This is what I believe is essential to success.

Too many voices can have you confused, but the voice who is attached to your assignment can take you there unhindered. Find the right church that is right for you to fulfill your purpose. I believe my journey as an entrepreneur is a journey of ministry. Business has been a tool for me to minister to others. Through launching various businesses on my journey of becoming a SHERO, I have realized that entrepreneurship is a lifestyle for me.

Stay Connected to the Source So You Can Move with Zeal!

"NOT NOW! NOT LIKE THIS!"
~Ebony Walker~

———————•❖•———————

One of my favorite scriptures, no matter what I am going through, is Romans 8:28. The King James Version says; *"And we know that all things work together for good to them that love God, to them who are the called according to His purpose."*

When I say that this scripture has been my lifeline, believe it. It has been the compass needed in every decision I have made. It has highlighted the course that I needed to take, even when I honestly did not want to. It has realigned my focus amid turmoil and confusion. But most importantly, it has helped me to see beyond my natural vision. Because the truth is that life has a way of dumping things on you. Some, you were prepared for; some, you were not. Nevertheless, you must embrace the reality of all things working for your good; and this includes the "sucky" things. I can recall a "sucky" day when life dumped a pink slip on me – and I was not ready.

I worked approximately 20 minutes from my home. One day, I found myself with the option of calling out – due to snow and ice on the roads – or leaving home earlier to make it in on time. I decided to go to work. I decided to do my part, to bring home a nice paycheck. I decided to be the good lil' wife, who was trying to make a good name for herself in Corporate America while helping my husband provide for our family. Yes, I was doing what I was supposed to be doing. But here is where the problem lies; to do what I felt I was supposed to do, I completely ignored what God told me to do! It was several months prior to this time that God had been nudging me to start my own business. Naturally, a plethora of questions and concerns flooded my brain simultaneously. This pushed me right in the grips of disobedience.

It pushed me towards being comfortable with this bi-weekly paycheck. It pushed me towards deciding that now was not the time to step out. Therefore, I was allowed to walk in disobedience. (I know that is not popular, but there are times when God will give you exactly what you want – even when it is not the best for you!). But imagine my surprise when I was fired from this extremely beneficial job, almost 4 weeks later, for clocking in ONE MINUTE LATE on the snow day that I chose to come in on. The shock and anger that ran through me, as I was called into the office that evening, after completing my shift, was like a rage I had not felt before. And unbeknownst to me, there was talk of budget cuts and layoffs. However, I was making this company some VERY good money. There was NO way that I would be on the chopping block. The joke was proven to be on me when I was asked to clock out and turn in my badge – never to return. Yep, I admit it – I broke down. I cried. I was furious. I was making good money and was excited about being able to help my husband take care of our home. But in the blink of an eye, that was snatched from me. How was I to be a helpmate if I was not financially helping my mate?

Not NOW! Not like THIS! There is NO way that this is right. How dare they let ME go? I was one of their top producers and always stayed for overtime if needed. I was not full of drama or gossip. If I had an appointment, I provided legal and acceptable documentation. So, why me? Why now? Why like this? Then I heard a voice, a familiar voice, which gave me the answer: "If only you had left when I told you, instead of trusting your fears." Trusting my fears? Is THAT what I was doing? Yes, I was in full denial with that statement because there is no way that God could be talking to me or about me! Nah, not ME! But yes, beloved, it was I. I was the problem, I was the enemy to myself, and I was the hold up. And to add insult to injury, I had lost the business idea that He had given me several months prior. Could not even remember fully what He had shown me. So, I was stuck!

No creativity, no plan, no desire, no nothing! Then the spirit of depression hit me. My degree meant absolutely nothing. I could not get a job anywhere, I could not get government assistance, I could not get unemployment, and I had to accept that it was my fault. It is crazy how one "minIscule" act of disobedience, even when assumed to be light or insubstantial, can shift the dynamics and direction of purpose. It can cause time to stop and make us look at what we could have had if we had been compliant. So, when I say suffering was my portion, it was for a season.

I applied for jobs that I never imagined working, only to get rejected. I went on interviews and had people who knew people that could help me. But nothing worked. "How is this, God? Why would you allow my efforts to be made in vain?" I had the nerve to ask Him why I was suffering when I clearly set myself up for this. And one day, I had to be honest. I had to tell the truth – to ME! I had to say, "God, I repent! Please help me fix this because I am not supposed to be struggling like this. Help me to trust You." And in that instance, He took me to the scripture of John 13:7. The Amplified version states, "...You do not realize now what I am doing, but you will [fully] understand it later."

Come on, God. Not NOW! NOT like THIS! There HAD to be a better way. My husband was having health issues, we needed to move, we needed a vehicle that would not break down monthly, my son was a growing pre-teen with needs, AND we were in ministry – paying the bulk of the church bills from the little that we had. We had to pawn things, we had to borrow, we had to do "rock, paper, scissors" to see which bill was getting paid this week and who we would request an extension from. I remember many days saying, "I didn't sign up for this!" But even in this discomfort, in this aggravation, with this thorn, ALL things were working! Because it was in this place where excuses had to expire, and innovation had to resurrect. Yes, innovation was there all along; however, I had buried it under anger. I had buried it under pity. I had buried it under excuses. I had buried it under the blame game. I had buried it under my own disdain for myself. And one day, the curse was broken. But it could only break when I decided to stop piling my issues on top of my reality! The issue was that I was experiencing lack, but the reality is that it could have been prevented if I would have just trusted God as much as I preached about doing so! That is when the shift occurred.

One day, I woke up and verbally declared that a new way of thinking was my lifestyle. I declared that a new way of bringing consistent financial increase was going to meet me where I was. And since faith without works is dead, I started looking for it and preparing for it while I was expecting it. I was intentional. I tried to do MLM (multi-level marketing) and tried to sell things that everyone else was selling, which appeared to be prosperous. From customized shirts to shoes, from weight loss supplements to other health and wellness products – I tried! But it just was not me. And I had to accept that I was steadily trying to force myself into a puzzle that I did not fit. I so desperately wanted the success that I saw in my business partners. I wanted to be the girl who would walk the stage and get the big checks and rank up quickly. But that was not part of my story or my destiny. Yes, prosperity was and is on me; however, it had to come through the gifts that God gave me. And this was NOT the way! So, one day, I began to write.

I have always been a writer and always kept journals. I have been writing poems and short stories and songs since the age of seven. But it was in this moment that passion was flowing through my fingertips and powerful words were coming to mind quicker than I could pen them. Suddenly, I heard that same familiar voice tell me, "This is what you were created to do – write!" IT SCARED ME! I stopped in mid-sentence and was suddenly hit with a light bulb idea: "How do I become a ghostwriter? Do people even pay someone else to write their stuff?" And so, I decided to do a quick Google search. That was in 2016 – and my world changed. I never looked back!

I joined a few online platforms that would allow me to create profiles and become a "Ghostwriter for Hire" or a "Freelancer." Overtime, my clientele list grew, and many referred me to their network. I went from writing a couple of speeches per week to writing books and website content and newsletter communications daily. I went from writing wedding vows and poems to writing jingles for major companies. Finally, I was in my element. And yes, I was doing something I loved!

As a child, I was deemed to be a prophetic scribe. And while I had no idea the magnitude of such an assignment, I now understand the power of my spoken and written words. In 2018, I officially stepped out and launched Walk UpWrite. With this platform, I provide writing services – of all calibers – that are upright. Honest. Creative. Plagiarism free. And yes, I pray before each assignment and ask God for wisdom to write.

Since its birth, I have been able to help others manifest – which is one of my favorite words! I have been given seeds to ideas locked behind brilliant minds and created books and curriculums that have catapulted multitudes into destiny. Some have asked if it bothers me to be a ghost. But on the contrary, I love pushing others forward from behind the scenes. I have learned that your gift will ALWAYS make room for you, no matter what that gift might be. And when you operate in it from a pure place, NO good thing will God withhold from you. So, all the books, autobiographies, jingles, newsletters, press releases, speeches, wedding vows, website content, marketing material, and even the sermons – yes, I am blessed to have helped people across the globe say what they need to say. And the truth is that I love operating for an Audience of One.

You see, if I do what God has purposed me to do with my gift then that is ALL that matters! Yes, it takes discipline and humility to not get the "big head" when you gain Hollywood entertainers or well-known politicians as clients. But in those times, I remember that it is NEVER about me and it never will be! It is, however, about infiltrating the world with the beauty of obedience. It is about showing other women, other people, that obedience is better than sacrifice. It is about letting my gift make room for me and properly position me. This is the essence of becoming a Shero. By definition, a "hero" is courageous and noble. They are often regarded as a role model. And being a Shero is doing exactly that – but in heels! Still, I can only be a role model if I model the walk of obedience and faith. And at this very moment, I want to encourage you to do the same.

Nobody can EVER beat you at being you! Therefore, strive to be you with all your might. Walk in your calling, no matter who understands or disapproves. Listen to the reminders and adhere to the gentle nudges. Why? Because creation awaits you, according to Romans 8:19. And the very last thing you need to do is make the graveyard rich. So please, do not die full. Your mandate is to live full and die empty. When you leave this world, everything that is inside of you should be poured out in some capacity. And if you do not personally manifest it, the vision should be written so that someone else can read it and run with it (according to Habakkuk 2:2). Either way, you must release it!

Today, I am a devoted wife, supportive mother, an intentional intercessor, a bestselling author, and a successful entrepreneur. With all of that in mind, I can boldly state Romans 8:28 in a more personalized way: And I know that EVERY SINGLE THING concerning God's Will for my life has worked EXACTLY as it needed to. And that is because I love Him, I am called by Him, and my purpose is IN Him! So yes, I know.

ALL things work – even when you are having a "not now" or a "not like this" moment.

SHEROES EMBRACE
THE PIVOT

A pivot is a change in strategy without a change in vision.

~ Eric Ries ~

EMBRACING ME
~Latoya S. Harrington~

I remember a time of being fragile and broken, a time where the words, thoughts, and actions of others would make or break me. How was I supposed to be happy? How was I supposed to live my best life pleasing and doing what everyone else wanted me to do? What about Toya? What about my dreams and my aspirations and believe me they were BIG dreams and BIG aspirations?

I have always been one to take chances but why did I need approval from others so bad before moving forward. For years, I contemplated what I wanted to do with my life. I always had this idea of becoming a doctor or a nurse. Eventually time went by and I graduated from King's College in 2008 with a degree in Medical Assisting. I worked as a Medical Assistant for 8 years and I just knew I had found my "thing". I loved patient care and I was good at what I did.

Becoming a medical assistant was the next best thing to being a nurse, so I thought. There seemed to always be something missing. I would work this 9-5 job, come home, be a mom, be a wife, and the cycle would continue. Every day it was the same thing. My creative mind was in jail. I was doing what everyone else wanted me to do. Work a job; make money take care of my home, go to church blah blah blah... I know, I know these are typical requirements of being a mother and an adult but what happened to loving what you do?

I heard someone say when you love what you do you will never work a day in your life. I was ready to try something new. I started out decorating/coordinating events and parties at the office and finally! I was able to let my creative juices flow. I had begun to tap into my purpose.

In September 2015, my husband surprised me with 3 amazing birthday/anniversary gifts; a sewing machine, an embroidery machine, and a custom cutting machine. I was clearly in creative heaven. It is always a blessing when your spouse is your number one supporter. Little did he know that was the beginning of something great? A seed had been planted that day and I was determined for it to grow. I had no clue how to operate any of them, but hey how hard could it be?

I would rush home excited and ready to play with my machines. Watching tutorials and reading books and articles during my lunch break had become the new normal for me. I tell anyone that when you really want to achieve something you must be willing to put in the work. It is easy to just say a thing, but it is harder to put action with it. Faith without works is dead.

For many weeks of trial and error I learned how to sew. I had made my first infinity scarf and I was ecstatic. It took me every bit of 2 hours to make. Thinking back, it is so funny to me considering I can make one now in 10 minutes.

I was so focused and determined to get this thing right. I devoted my time, my energy, and my thoughts to starting my own sewing business. I was going to make scarves. Team scarves, fleece scarves, infinity scarves, character scarves, you name it, I was the scarf girl. Something so simple becomes a business.

I learned early on that if I was going to make this work, I had to retrain my way of thinking. I could no longer allow the thoughts and opinions of others to dictate what I did or did not do. You cannot expect people to see what you see. They saw a little scarf business: I saw something much greater. Many days I would work my full-time job and come home and work the business full time. Early mornings and late nights were the story of my life. You cannot expect to withdraw from something you have not deposited into. I deposited a lot of time and a lot of money. You must know that being your own boss is much more difficult than being an employee. As my skill set grew, I grew, and my business grew.

Customers would begin to challenge my skills by requesting things I had never made before. See when people are really for you and want to see you win, they will challenge and push you to heights you probably would never go alone. As an entrepreneur there should not be a time that you become comfortable where you are. Yes, you learn and grow and become more confident in what you are doing, but you should always be looking for the next thing. Learn something new, try something different.

Being a BOSS is a Faith Walk. Without faith in me or faith in God none of what I have accomplished would have been possible. It is important that you connect and link up with positive people. I have heard people say I did this by myself with no help and I do not need anyone. For a while I worked alone. Just me, myself and I ran the business. I did absolutely everything and after some time, it became a bit much. How can you expect to grow alone? You cannot. You need to have a team of people to help and support you. I soon came to realize that I was insecure, selfish, and stuck, and while that may seem like a harsh thing to say about yourself, it was the truth. I was the hold up of my own success.

It is not always easy to recognize when it is you that is holding you up. Sometimes you must step back and evaluate yourself, your atmosphere, and your business. Embracing who I was became a big part of my business and ministry. I began to realize that if I put a cap on who was, I would never truly reach my full potential in life or business. It is so easy to blame others for our failures and mess ups. "My business isn't growing because my family doesn't support me." "My business isn't growing because my friends aren't buying from me." Your business success is not dependent upon your family and friends' support. Your business success is based on you and what you do for your business. Your business, Your brand. When I got that in my heart and in my mind, my thoughts and my actions began to change. With this change, my little scarf business turned into a growing and thriving sewing business. I went from making scarves to sewing custom gowns, dresses, and clergy robes.

It took time and perseverance to level up. When I think back to when I created my first dress, the seams were off, the zipper was tacky, and it looked a complete mess, but I was determined to still wear and wear it proudly. I said that to say, you may not get it right the first time or even the second or third time, but do not give up. Perfect and research your craft. That makes the difference by itself. Since starting in 2015, SEW FAB & Company has become a ministry as well. In 2018, we were able to debut our very first dramatic runway show. Telling a story of how a young lady goes from being fragile to fabulous and how God transformed her life. That young lady is me. As a part of my ministry and business I make it my business to encourage and mentor young women who were like me at one point.

I can remember not liking myself or loving myself to the point where I tried to commit suicide. I have since then, embraced everything about my past and present that has created the women I am today. Use your life experience to build your brand. Let it be what fuels and pushes you to greater heights. Let the haters hate and the naysayers say what they will. It will only make you stronger.

Looking back to when I first started in one of our small spare bedrooms to now having my own building, I am an example of progress and success. You can throw every excuse out there as to why you are not where you want to be, but let us be honest. Who is in control of your life? I have not made the progress I have made by making excuses and procrastinating.

Do when no one else does. Work when everyone else is asleep, move when everyone else is standing still, go when no one else will go. My motto for SEW FAB is why blend in when you were created to stand out. Embrace who and whose you are. That is what will set you apart as a business and brand. There is no other like you.

Psalms 139:14 says, *I praise you because I am fearfully and wonderfully made; your works are wonderful; I know that full well.*

I have embraced this journey and it is well worth the ride. Clearly, I can see who He has called me to be. I am fearless and wonderfully made and I am Embracing Me.

SURVIVING WITH PLAN B
~AnneMarie Ziegler~

As women we usually have a Plan B tucked into the side pocket of our purse or the back pocket of our jeans. We realize, no matter how much we prep and plan, that something will come up and not go as expected. Thus, we have Plan B ready to pull out, so we can keep moving forward.

Most of us probably had a plan growing up as to what our lives would be like, the college we would attend, the career, the type of spouse or not, where we would live, and if we would have children and how many. I had those plans; they were made at an early age and were wrapped up in a pretty box with a lovely bow! My plans derailed incredibly early, and I quickly figured I needed to keep a Plan B handy!

Thinking back on my life, I realize (and admit) I was attacked by a visiting relative, I was raped by a family friend, I became a widow with four children early in life, I was physically abused, homeless, worked for a manipulative and verbally abusive boss, got swindled out of a house we were buying by a shady real estate agent, to name a few of my departures from the road I had planned on traveling. Yet, I have pulled out Plan B each time and survived all of it, with the goal being to stay positive and keep moving forward.

I was married at 17. No work, no college and at 21 my first child was born. During the next nine years, I had three more children, worked various jobs, attended college on and off, and finally began a career that I loved. I thought to myself, "Okay, a different path with lots of detours, but back on the plan." Just as the future was looking brighter, my husband Charles got injured on the job. He survived a fall from two and a half stories, with multiple injuries, and was sent home that same day from the hospital. After three days of making phone calls, he was finally admitted into the hospital for multiple broken bones and internal injuries.

There were countless medical visits, therapy, referrals, loss of income and he had a botched surgery which left him partially paralyzed. According to the Contractor, the accident was not anyone's fault as he was a construction worker who worked for a subcontractor, who worked for a subcontractor, who worked for a contractor, who worked for a large corporation. The six of us worked together, tightening belts that were already tight, but not complaining, and knowing there would be a better outcome for us, somewhere down the road.

As they prepared my husband for another surgery, he was diagnosed with Stage 4 lung cancer. While in my early forties with four children, I found myself a widow. This was certainly not in any plan I had! I had recently finished my degree in Respiratory Therapy and was working at a regional Trauma Center. This detour not only affected me but also our four children. We all adjusted and took various paths, moving and living in different places over the next few years. Certainly not a plan any of us had envisioned, sometimes losing touch with each other, but always coming back together when one of us needed it. We survived it and never used it as an excuse.

As I began a new life, I met a man that seemed to care deeply for me. I worked in his business and helped him to grow it. Little did I realize it, but slowly over the seven years we were together, he had begun abusing me. First, it was psychologically, then financially, verbally, and finally physically. I was admitted to the hospital due to injuries, and my children were there for me. Being homeless, I spent a long weekend with my daughter who lived a couple of hours from where I lived and worked. My youngest son and his family lived in a town near me and took me in, so I would have someplace to live. After a few weeks of sleeping on the floor there, I moved into my own place. Not one to stay down for long, I was given the opportunity to do some volunteer work for an international domestic violence organization. I was able to help others get out of domestic violence situations, offer comfort, understanding, a shoulder, and knowledge. As I traveled throughout the Southeast giving presentations, I was also able to help others see this situation does not just happen to uneducated, naïve, dependent women. I had a job and education, and there was nothing dependent about me. I was even able to do some consulting with the Chicago Police Department on a high-profile case that involved domestic violence. I gave hope and inspired others to leave their situation and seek the resources that may have possibly saved their lives. If you have something to happen to you and you ask "Why?" ... Well, this was my "why" I took a bad situation and turned it into something positive. I was not a victim, but a survivor.

I met Paul, my current husband, who has stood by my side during many difficult times. A year after we were married, he started having some problems with his balance. After several doctor visits and lots of tests at Duke and UNC-Chapel Hill Hospitals, we learned he had a degenerative neurological disorder, which has no treatment or cure. From that point forward, he was unable to work. Paul and I moved back to my home to be near my family. At one point, he was in a wheelchair and unable to walk on his own. Again, the family rallied around, and we moved forward, with lots of ups and downs and lots of help to care for Paul.

After a couple of jobs, I started my own business, in a very male-dominated field. I am blessed to have two female friends in various parts of the state who are also publishers, who I can seek advice and words of wisdom from them, as there is no support locally. I have been fortuitous to have made some wonderful friends and colleagues, who have been by my side and have had my back to help me make our magazines top notch. They have joined with me in other projects as well, always being the great cheerleaders needed along the road.

Many have been strong, independent women, and there have been some real gentlemen (not just men), and I am proud to call all of them "friend," as well as my family always being there to help.

There are times when I felt like the little kitten hanging on for dear life on that poster, but I know I can always ask for help from one of my children or one of my many amazing friends. Without the support of family and friends, I would not be where I am today with my business, or in my life. Isn't that what we all strive for? Aren't they the ones who make us a "shero?" I know whatever happens that I will not be a victim, but a survivor, and I will always look for ways to be positive and to help those around me, and my community. I hope to not point fingers but to be able to offer solutions.

Having traveled from one side of the state to the other and back home again, I have had a chance to stop and look back at my life and the challenges and struggles I have faced. I have learned to draw from the teachings of my two grandmothers, one from the South and one from the North. They were both extraordinarily strong and intelligent women who spoke their minds and had vastly different outlooks on life, yet they were also remarkably similar. I feel fortunate to have spent so much time with them both, able to learn so much from them.

My mother always worked in the financial sector, while the other mothers stayed at home and baked cookies. I never missed out on her cookies, as she was another strong female role model for me. I had three aunts who I always looked up to, and they were all strong independent women, who did not follow the norm. I am extremely fortunate to have had such strong independent women in my life, amazing children, a husband that encourages me, and friends that I can reach out to any time of the day or night. They give me the courage and encouragement to live outside of the box, speak my mind, be independent and strong, and to be a survivor, who keeps Plan B tucked away in a side pocket. They also taught me that some days, after you have used Plan A and then Plan B, to be grateful there are twenty-four more letters in the alphabet!

OPENED DOOR
~Dr. Michelle Vann~

Kurt Carr penned a song called For Every Mountain that I believe so uniquely expresses my journey. As I look over the many blessings and the open doors that have been presented to me, all I can say is it was the Lord that truly made a way for me to be where I am today.

As I look over the many blessings and open doors that have been presented to me, all I can say is that it was you, Lord, that made a way. From the rejection of being an unwanted and unplanned pregnancy to the present moment, I can see God's hand at work in my life. Despite being unwanted and unplanned, my mother chose to give birth to me. While this came with its challenges, God was there. My great aunt and uncle loved me and kept me available to my mom but gave me the stability I needed. I walked through this open door before I had the wherewithal to know. A little complicated to understand but imagine how confused I was as a kid.

As I grew, God continued to place people in my life that led me to knowledge, wisdom, and spiritual growth, igniting the teacher in me. I knew from childhood that teaching and preaching were a part of who I am. From playing church on the farm to gathering my stuffed animals into a classroom for a lesson, I knew the call but needed guidance.

While seeking and listening for direction I met my future husband. Picture it. Sicily, 1990 … wait this is not Golden Girls. Ok, it was 1990 and I met this young man with a dapper haircut and the shiniest teeth. He was a smooth talker and kind of floated as he walked. He had swagger and a bit of arrogance. Not enough to turn you off but put you on notice. As we talked, I always told him that I hoped he found a wife that could put up with his big talk and large ideas.

He and his buddy, David, always called themselves "Upwardly mobile and Urban contemporary men." This was a phrase that exemplified how they saw themselves. Larger than life and ready for anything that came their way. He saw potential in us doing big things together. This big thinking led him to ask my grandpa and my daddy/uncle for my hand in marriage. Seriously? Get married? Us? Hmm, what an idea! The thing that pushed me over the edge was the check he wrote. He gave me a laminated check for one lifetime of Love and Happiness signed by him. How could I say no?

If you know anything about fleecing God (this is just asking God to show you something tangible so that you know the answer is from him) for answers, then you have seen my name next to the definition. I am a fleecer. William had asked but I needed to know – without a shadow of a doubt – that this was God. I prayed, Lord if this is my husband make every light from my house to my job be green.

I lived in Ark City and worked in Winfield, 15 or so miles away. Every light was green! Ok, Lord that could have been a fluke. Do it on the way home. Every light was green. Wow! Okay, God, that was freaky, but I hear you. Ok, one more thing. I want someone to come and speak to me about this marriage that knows nothing about the proposal and when they are finished, I will have total peace. My cousin's maternal aunt was in town and asked me to come and roll up her hair. I did not know why me but when we say yes, God works. She and I were talking and sharing, and someone came through and shared that I was getting married. She inquired about our upcoming nuptials and I shared with her my concerns and the backlash I was getting (we are from two different Pentecostal denominations that thought the other was not "saved"). She smiled and said, "Honey, I totally understand. Let me tell you about what happened to me …"

I will not share her story because it is hers, but I will tell you that when she finished, I felt the peace of God sweep over my body and knew she was the answer to my fleece. I had my three confirmations and was off to get married. These situations did not happen by chance. When we seek him, God opens doors and gives answers.

I told you William is a big thinker. He went to the public library and read a book called The Electroplater's Handbook. After reading it, he came home and said, "We are going into business." Ok, how do we do that? This was new. Neither of us had been in business like this on our own. This was a big move. The next week a magazine came to our house with an electroplating do-it-yourself kit in it. It was cool but we did not have the money. We had just gotten married. We put it aside saying if this is supposed to happen, God will make a way. A few weeks later we went to New Mexico for a honeymoon/church conference. When you grow up Pentecostal, church conferences were our vacations! One night the preacher said, "Get in your mind what you want God to do for you and your family and speak it." We agreed that we wanted God to give us the money to start this business. The very next week we received a live check in the mail from American General Financial Service for the amount that we needed. All we had to do was sign the back of the check and return it. God is so good;one he added a little extra to the check for a business phone line in our house. We were in business!

We did a little practicing and went to a dealership to see if they would let us try our hand at gold plating, a technique where electric current adheres gold to other metal objects, on one of their cars. Remember, I told you I was married to a talker. He convinced that man to give us the emblems, the silver words, off that car then and there. We came home, plated them, and took them back the next day. They sold that beautiful black Diamante with gold emblems that same day. They were able to mark up our work by 50% and the door was kicked wide open. We were able to bring a touch of gold to a whole dealership chain. This business went forth and blessed our family for years.

While working this business my passion for education would not go out and I went back to school for my degree in education. Business was good but every entrepreneur needs a good teacher. I was not sure what grade I wanted to teach so I began to substitute. On a bright Thursday morning I walked into this lovely 5th-grade class and one of the students was a young lady with a full face of make-up. I found it odd but just chuckled. About an hour into the class, a small lady about 5'3", with big hair and an even bigger personality walked in the door and explained that she was the principal. She locked eyes on that same young lady and told her to go to the bathroom, wash her face, and then meet her in the office. Wow! I love you! This beautiful and powerful black woman called me the very next day and said, "I watched you yesterday and I like what I saw. I am creating a new classroom next week. I have already pulled your file and there are a few things you need to handle at HR. I will see you on Monday at 9 am. Have a good weekend."

And, like that, I had a job and a lifetime friend. Barbara Mackey will always be a part of what made me who I am today. Her guidance and resolute demeanor ignited the fire that I needed to pursue my new career. Do not get me wrong I have several teachers in my family that showed me the ropes, but she loved me when she did not have to, and for that I am grateful; which leads me to 2017 and my final year of teaching public school.

Throughout my teaching career, there were so many opportunities afforded to me that were the hand of God. I have never done all the right things, but I serve a right God; while teaching may not feel entrepreneurial; it one of the biggest opportunities to sow into the lives of entrepreneurs. I admit I had a blast with the kids over the years. The lives I was able to mold and impacts were countless. The seeds I dropped about how big the world is and how much you must contribute to it were priceless. It is funny when I see former students that became teachers, and they say that having a black teacher helped them know they could be a teacher as well. One might say that my teaching style is stern but loving. I am the auntie that will get you told but deep down you know you can share your heart with, and you will be guided in the right direction.

They go further to say they see why I was hard on them. I will not say that I always did everything perfectly, I am still human, but I did what I believed was right at the time.

The book of Ecclesiastes tells us that there is a time and a season for everything. And though I was a somewhat of "superhero" to the kiddos, the time had come to close the door on teaching and move on to what was next. I did not want to miss anything that God had for me in the future. In the book, Story of My Life, Helen Keller wrote, "When one door of happiness closes, another opens, but often we look so long at the closed door that we do not see the one which has been opened for us." I do not want to miss anything that God has for my future. I do not want you to miss anything that has your name on it. Whatever God is doing in this season, do not allow it to happen without you. I know that God has opened doors for each of us, but we must knock, seek, and open the door designed specifically for us.

I pray that you ask God to open the eyes of your understanding so that you can see, hear, and know his plan for your future. Sis, I am, and you are, a Shero. Live Blessed!

FINDING MYSELF
~Dr. Belinda Wilkerson~

I lost myself and I was miserable. In relocating seven hundred and twenty-four miles from the place that nurtured me, educated me, and grew me up, I could not find myself. A die-hard New Englander in her late fifties moving to the South, I butted heads with culture shock. A lifelong educator who loved her students and found her purpose in education did not have a job. For the first time since I was six, I was not connected to a place of education; that rocked me to my core. No professional network.

I missed having daily conversations with colleagues about educating students, whether at the secondary or post-secondary level, those conversations fueled me to want to do better for my students and for my profession. People rejoice in becoming empty nesters. They plan for the days when they can convert that extra bedroom into an office space or a craft room. I did not. Mothering my two sons brought a joy like no other – it still does. But they were not moving with us and the empty hole from their daily absence remains unfilled.

What do you do when you spend all day doing retail therapy and as you are driving home you realize not one person spoke your name? That verse from the Cheers television show rolled around in my head as tears welled up and the ugly cry began:

If you ever watched Cheers, you know the verse to which I'm referring. Everyone knows you, they're happy to see you and the conversation is good. Yes, that verse sent me into a dark place that day.

It is not that I did not look for a job; no one would hire me at any of the colleges to which I applied. Most of the time my applications for positions such as academic advisor, career advisor and such, were not acknowledged. A soul-sucking silence was the most common response. The last time I had difficulty finding meaningful work was back in 1975 after graduating from Rhode Island College with a teaching degree in History. After working in public education for 30+ years, with little autonomy over the curriculum, working as the Counselor-in-Residence for The Rhode Island School Counseling Project at Providence College for six years with full autonomy to use my skills and knowledge to shape a program working with school counselors and district administrators, I gained more confidence in my ability to be a leader and to make decisions on programming. Returning to any public-school system after those glorious years of freedom was not part of my plan. I had to figure something out; there were too many firsts (no kids, no friends, no job, no Rhode Island comfort foods) and I was sinking further into that headspace of wondering whether I mattered or not. During one of my five trips home in that first year, one of my trusted colleagues in higher education said, "Put your big girl panties on and do something different." She suggested I become an independent educational consultant (IEC). What! That was blasphemy. She wanted me to go from being a professional school counselor to an IEC. Traditionally, school counselors and IECs have had a cool relationship; school counselors believed IECs charged exorbitant fees and worked exclusively with affluent families while calling into question the capability of the school counselor to meet the needs of their college bound students. On the other hand, IECs felt misrepresented and did not understand why we could not all just get along.

Thank God that narrative is evolving into a positive dialogue.

I knew I had to do something besides retail therapy and traveling home to Rhode Island frequently. Heeding the words of my esteemed colleague, I stepped out on faith and researched the path to becoming an independent educational consultant. After attending a workshop, Transitioning to Private Practice, at the National Association for College Admission Counseling (NACAC) annual conference, I saw glimmers of hope. The Independent Educational Consultants Association (IECA), headed by Mark Sklarow who facilitated this workshop, helped me discover another way to transfer my skills and knowledge as a teacher, school counselor and college instructor. The scary part was, I had no training in running a business and becoming an independent educational consultant meant I had to develop new skills and knowledge in running a business. So many times, especially during the early years, that voice in my head would shout, "Just retire from work!" but I was not cut out to be a housewife. Besides, work gives meaning to my life and if I felt there was value in my work, I was not retiring.

IECA conducts a Summer Training Institute (STI) to introduce newer consultants to the entrepreneurship side of the work, in addition to best practices for consulting. To jumpstart my business, my plan was to attend the 2011 STI; however, friends from home scheduled a visit during the same week. Not wanting to lose momentum, I sought out and hired a mentor for six months to walk me through setting up a business. A former school counselor who transitioned to consulting several years prior, Rebecca, guided me through setting up an LLC, applying for an employee identification number (EIN) and myriad required tasks. Before my work began with her, I needed a name for my company. How do you pick a name when entrepreneurship was never a thought? I asked three RI friends in counseling to help me pick a name. Through a process of conversation and elimination, 'Steps to The Future' was born. In hindsight, I might have added college counseling to the name to brand the type of service offered by my new company. Next step was a logo. One of the perks of being a high school counselor is working with talented students. I knew a student from my former high school now worked as a graphic designer and I reached out to her to design my logo.

She did not disappoint. After several iterations, I chose the design and colors you see on all my materials. Now, I needed a website. Again, I reached out to a former student, had multiple email communications about my vision and before the Fall of 2011 ended; I had my fledging business up and running. While I was creating my business, I was honing my skills as a community volunteer and increasing my knowledge in the field of career development. Having taught the Career Information class for the master's level Counselor Education Program at Providence College, I had my sights set on receiving a certificate as a Global Career Development Facilitator (GCDF). Becoming a GCDF required three components: education, experience, and coursework. Lacking only the last component, I registered for the course, which was conducted mostly online. Several lessons mandated in person attendance and I enjoyed meeting new professionals for the networking and the knowledge. That was a wonderful experience.

I also committed to learning more about the community I lived in. Who were these people in Cumberland County? What did they value? What brought them joy? What challenged them? I needed to know so I could figure out where I belonged in this community instead of feeling like a square peg in a round hole. I had to get out of the house to find out more. After several fits and starts, I became a volunteer at the Child Advocacy Center (CAC), an agency dedicated to advocating for the prevention of child sexual abuse. I still volunteer there occasionally, mainly to help at one of their annual fundraisers, but at one time, people thought I was employed there because I spent more time there than working on my business. Then, indulging in my lifelong love affair with books, I started volunteering at an afterschool teen program dispensing college and career information to middle and high school students. Kids, especially other peoples' kids, will keep you connected and challenged when you step into their world. To this day, this is one of the best moments of my week.

One important lesson I learned transitioning from public school employee to entrepreneur is the value of networking. Networking events used to make my skin crawl! The whole thought of entering a large, crowded room, making small talk with semi-strangers, and exchanging business cards did not appeal to my introverted nature. Networking as a teacher focused on exchanging curricula ideas, not marketing your brand. Attending a variety of business- focused workshops through Fayetteville Technical Community College's (FTCC) 1 Million Cups and local women's networking groups helped me understand how to network properly. I strongly recommend new entrepreneurs seek out resources in their community such as their community college and beyond to assist them with learning about running a business - everything from identifying your target audience, to marketing, to the business practices required for annual reports. Connecting with FTCC's Center for Innovation & Entrepreneurship has provided me and other local business owners with expert advice at no cost.

I continue to explore ways to connect within our community. As a business owner, I have learned the importance of creating a space for myself outside of the confines of the business by giving back to my community. I love books and fortune allowed me to serve on the Board of Trustees for our local library system. Introducing young folks to the programs and resources available to them with a library card brings me joy. When given the opportunity, I speak with young people about the transformative power of an education. As a first-generation college student, I know that education, a life- long endeavor for me, makes a difference.

Malcolm X said, "Education is the passport to the future, for tomorrow belongs to those who prepare for it today."

On my journey to finding myself, I am grateful for the silver linings in the dark clouds that once hovered overhead. Attending the Summer Training Institute in 2012 introduced me to Antoinette Battiste, affectionately known as "my twin". Our friendship sustains me in moments of despair and elevates my soul to the highest levels of joy on many days. I found a community of like-minded colleagues who inspire, motivate, and empower students daily. Collaborating with them strengthens my resolve to use my business to bring value to my students and their families. After almost a decade as an entrepreneur, I continue to uncover those silver linings and use these words by Martin Luther King, Jr., to guide me –

"Faith is taking the first step even when you don't see the whole staircase."

SHEROES THINK DIFFERENTLY

"*Thoughts have power. Thoughts are energy. You can make your world or break it by your own thinking.*"

~ Susan Taylor ~

WHEN YOU FEEL LIKE A FRAUD
~Cheryl S. (Cherie) Hall~

Have you ever felt this way? You know all the right things to do, all the right things to say, and you even know the steps to take (i.e., set a goal, have action steps that are measurable, etc.); yet you find yourself from day to day looking at the list and doing nothing. I call that, "Feeling like a fraud," and if you are not careful, you will find yourself going down a rabbit hole you cannot get out of. But wait; before I get into all that, I guess I should introduce and tell you a little bit about myself.

My name is Cheryl S. (Cherie) Hall, and my journey to entrepreneurship is a bit unorthodox. Becoming an entrepreneur was not originally on my radar, at least, not in the traditional way you think about. I sing, and that was to be my career choice. I had enrolled in what was then Memphis State University, and I had successfully auditioned for the chorus. The professor had outlined the plan for touring Spain in the spring, and I was excited about all the possibilities that would bring. Unfortunately, a bad case of strep throat, followed by pneumonia (which resulted in a hospital stay of almost a week), caused me to put that path on hold. So, I went to my second love and built a nice career in Office Administration. I eventually worked my way up into management after beginning a career in non-profit services. I really thought I would never leave that life, but sometimes, things do not go the way you plan.

After having my second child, and initially returning to work, it became clear that I wanted and needed something different. So, while I was on maternity leave, I began looking at different ways that I could become an entrepreneur. My love for singing was still there, and thanks to some gigs here and there, I again thought of ways I could make that love my career. I would get offered background or studio gigs, and I held out hope that those would lead to the goal of being on the road full time, both in the US and abroad. I love to harmonize and enjoy the synergy of creating music with others. However, trying to break into that industry was not as simple as I thought it would be. After a few starts (and stops), I began searching for possible careers I could have on my own terms. I created Cherie's World and launched an online wholesale store. My husband had inspired the name choice, probably a year or so prior to that, when I was pursuing music. This time, I sought a business that could "sell itself", so to speak. Of course, how many of you know that you need to make people aware of the fact that you HAVE a product that is available, before it can "sell itself?"

That led into my becoming a beauty consultant. I was first a user of the product, but never saw myself making this a business. My eventual Director always left the door open for whenever I was ready, which turned out to be five years later, AFTER she moved to another city. I strive to be a woman of my word, and I had said that if I ever decided to give the beauty business a try, I would contact her. That was over 15 years ago, and I am still a consultant. But there was one more love in my life . . . travel. My mom gave me the travel bug when I was a little girl. I wanted to see practically everything! I loved train travel and wanted to experience locations I had only read about in books. And if it put me near the water, it had my heart. I cannot swim, but it does not matter. Just to hear and see the waves is all the Zen I need. It is still my happy place!

So almost six years ago, thanks to a friend who knew I loved travel, I became a Travel Advisor, and I would not change a thing. Getting to learn more about the industry was very eye opening and really expanded my knowledge. The travel arena is vaster and more intricate than I could have ever imagined. Learning how I could shape this industry to fit my interests was amazing. Even though my specialty became cruises and coastal getaways (my happy place!), I like to say I am a Destination Specialist because all segments of the travel industry intrigue me. Whether it is a cruise or safari, or anywhere in between, I will help anyone with their travel plans.

It was about this time that all the thoughts God had been giving me about how Cherie's World could become its own entity, and not just a name I use, really began to take shape. Not only is Cherie's World the sum parts of me, but it also really began shaping itself as a business of its own. Product ideas, themes, collaborations; it all began to come together, and I went to work. I revamped the website and made the domain name be more than just a mask pointing to my beauty site or music site. I created a full website that now encompasses the best in Travel, Skincare and Cosmetics,

Entertainment and so much more. I began branding myself as Cherie's World as opposed to a consultant or a singer or whatever, separately. Cherie's World consists of all these things and more. I now travel here and abroad singing, acting as well as enjoying personal travel. I have even come full circle, and toured Spain with a Gospel Choir where we go each holiday season a week or so before Christmas and return about a week or so after the New Year. We have done this periodically over the last seven years. In addition, I have amazing clients in the travel and beauty industries and have collaborated with other business leaders to assist or refer them to the resources that they need. I wanted Cherie's World to feel like a community and safe place, where all are welcome.

But remember when I asked if you sometimes feel like a fraud? You post to social media; you share relevant and helpful information; you even accept challenges from your accountability partner(s) with a detailed plan of all the things you are going to accomplish by the end of the week. But on the inside, you feel lost. You know in theory where you need to start, but you do not move. You may feel overwhelmed. You may not feel worthy. You may feel like people do not want or need what you have to offer. You get on your conference calls and say all the right things, all the while knowing you have not done HALF the things that needed to be accomplished.

Well, I have news for you. You are not alone. If we are honest with ourselves, we have ALL felt like a "fraud", many days, but maybe just did not know what to call it. We are burned out, we have allowed someone or something to put a damper on our dreams, or we kept pushing, trying to ignore the fear or emptiness we were feeling inside, not realizing we may be on the verge of a breakdown. I believe we have been operating in the "Fake It 'Til You Make It" mode for so long, we think it's normal. I also think we take the "Never Let 'em See You Sweat" to the extreme sometimes; which eventually leads to us never really being honest with ourselves about where we are, and what we're doing. It can become a vicious cycle if we are not careful.

So where do we go from here? I often think of the scripture, Lamentations 3:23: Great is His faithfulness; His mercies begin afresh each morning (NLT). Just like His mercies are new every morning, we must remember that we start fresh every morning. Do our goals restart? No; but our action steps toward reaching those goals do. Do this: Break down your goals into monthly, weekly, and daily. Put measurable steps on each activity (i.e., I will finish this chapter before the end of the week! LOL!) Look at your list every day, several times a day if you must. Check off the ones you have finished and keep adding to your lists each day. There is always something to be done, and it is easier if you can see it in writing. Then the next question is probably, "How do I get inspired or motivated to move?"

Whew! That one can be tricky, but not impossible. Inspiration comes from outside sources, but motivation comes from within. You must motivate yourself to move, to get started, to keep going, to win. Inspiration can give you the jumpstart you need, but motivation helps you to keep going.

What inspires you? Is it music, spoken word, pictures, nature, your children? Whatever that "It" is, use that as your jumping point toward motivating yourself. For me, I have found that starting my day with music really gets me going. It makes me want to get out of bed each morning. Have I remembered to do it every day? No, I have not. But when I do, I see the difference it makes, and how productive I am on those days. How about you?

What makes you want to get out of bed each day? Find that "It", and then get moving. Set an alarm that speaks out loud, like a pill alarm. Set it for "speaking notification", and then make the title something that will either make you laugh or invigorate you to get going. Writing this just now reminded me to update my alarm. So, the next time it goes off, it is going to say, "Wake Yo' Butt Up! It's Time to Get Moving!!"

Whatever you use to inspire yourself, whatever your motivation is to move, know that you can do it. You have what you need to get it done. Even on those days you may feel like a fraud, look yourself in the mirror and say (yes, out loud – it is not silly), "I'm NOT a fraud. I have got this. I am a winner, no matter what it looks like or how I feel at this moment. I am authentically me. I have what people need, and I make a positive difference in the lives of others.

I AM A SHERO!"

GRACE BE WITH YOU

~Kim Meyers~

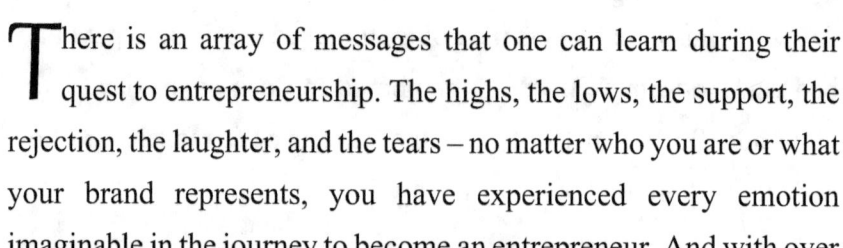

There is an array of messages that one can learn during their quest to entrepreneurship. The highs, the lows, the support, the rejection, the laughter, and the tears – no matter who you are or what your brand represents, you have experienced every emotion imaginable in the journey to become an entrepreneur. And with over 2 decades of experience, I can indisputably say that I have seen my share of it all. When asked to share nuggets as an accomplished entrepreneur, there are many directions I could travel. It is that it is hard to pick just a few.

I could talk about the financial gains afforded to me. I could talk about the independence and flexibility of being able to do things at my own pace. I even considered the power of being the conglomerate within my organization. All of these are highlights of the journey. But those on the outside must realize that they are only getting one view of the journey. However, the real deal is when nights comes. The real deal is when it is midnight, and the phones stop ringing. The real deal is when the orders stop popping up and the emails stop coming in. The real deal is when the conference calls are infrequent, and the invites are scarce. And yes, the friends and family who promised to support will become distant and invisible. You will find yourself being your sister's keeper for those who cannot keep their promises to you. And forget about wanting a celebration; you will have to become your own party planner, while trying to keep from having a pity party! All these statements were my reality. All of this became my painful truth. And while I could have given up, I could have allowed defeat to become part of my wardrobe, I made another decision. I embraced the Grace of God over my life and over the life of my business. When I tell you that it has made all the difference, please believe me. Because the truth is that I have NO idea where I would be, had it not been for Grace.

Allow me a moment to define this road that I call Grace. You see, it is two-dimensional and has been the catalyst to my success. You may hear the word "Grace", but you really do not understand how deep it goes for me. So, allow me to explain. As many of us know, God's Grace is when God gives us what we do not deserve. In conjunction with Grace is Mercy; this is when God does not give us what we deserve. And when the 2 are working on your behalf, you are experiencing a level of love that is indescribable. Again, I know for myself because it was Grace and Mercy that saved my business.

There was a point in my life when the doors deserved to close in my face. I wanted to do it all on my own terms and believed that I could figure things out. To put it bluntly, I was not coachable. Being coachable means that you are willing to learn. It means you must admit that you do not know it all and receive the wisdom and guidance of one who has more experience than you. Well, I was not quite there. And this should have turned out very tragic for me;

however, mercy met me where stubbornness resided. And God blessed my family financially in such a way that my mind and heart turned. But there was always Grace. And it was that Grace that God allowed to birth me into this world that helped me to see I was worth it. Grace loved me and gave me the affection I needed until I could love myself properly. Yes, mercy saved me and Grace kept me. Grace conceived me. Grace birthed me. Grace made me believe that I could become anything I set my heart and mind on. And so, I did.

Grace nurtured me when I was only days old, giving me her last name and vowing to protect me. Even when the next meal was nowhere in sight, Grace gave. She was the disciplinarian, the mother, the father, the protector, the encourager, and the one who cried for my happiness. Grace loved because she was love. And although Grace went home to be with The Lord in November of 2016, she will forever be in my heart. So, it is with that same Grace, God's Grace, that I am who I am today. But how did I become?

Unlike most people, becoming an entrepreneur was not something I was familiar with. That was not a popular term from my childhood, growing up in the city streets of New York. I was taught to go to school, get an education, and get a job. That word did not even exist in the conversations of my friends and me. Owning your own legitimate and legal business was more like a fairytale. So, if it is not embedded in you, how can you learn to appreciate or embrace it? When the idea was initially given to me, I gave an emphatic "NO!" There was NO way that I could want something I knew nothing about! So, working for someone else was my normal. It was what I knew. However, that mindset obviously changed one day. What I did not know, I became fluent in. What I once rejected; I fell in love with. What was once foreign to me became my well – the well that watered my family and me in such an undeniable way. Was it always easy? No! Did I have challenges? Absolutely! And getting over those challenges was difficult, but it was possible.

One of the greatest challenges in my journey was the death of my mother, my Grace. She was absolutely everything to me and her departure was the worst day of my life. It is crazy how one phone call can change the direction of your entire day. I remember waking up and feeling excited, I was in praise and worship, I knew it would be an amazing day. But around 1:37pm, a phone call reached me, and the piercing truth of darkness flew through the lines. She was gone. Just like that! I thought it was a joke. I hoped it was a prank. But a 2nd phone call from a Georgia State Trooper revealed the ugly truth. I lost control, I felt helpless, and I felt dead inside. Her death made me feel numb and made me feel like it was my life that was lost. This hurt me more than I can express. Talk about crying a river – no, I cried a tsunami. My family did all they knew to do to help me, to heal me, to usher me through this dark valley. And through it all, I can say that Grace did abound. Grace reminded me that I had purpose. Grace reminded me that the pain I was feeling was created to fuel my passion. There is a hymn that says, "Love lifted me." And that is true, but I would also like to sing, "Grace lifted me!"

Now, all that I do is to celebrate the life and legacy of my mother, Grace.

This journey has given me a platform for greatness. But when I started, I was young and immature. I thought everything was about me and I stood on platforms, showing off what I thought I knew – my education, my beauty, my ability to captivate. I was putting on a mask, showboating and trying to produce millions; however, I often failed to remember that it was NEVER about me and ALWAYS about God's people. I discovered that I was never going to get where I needed to be unless I reverted to the place of teaching, coaching, and training. Entrepreneurship was not going to be my call otherwise.

I found myself in a desert land. I knew nothing, although I thought I knew it all. I had nothing of value, although I thought I had it all. I was prepared for nothing, although I felt I was equipped for it all. And I was only fooling myself. This land was dry, hot, and miserable. I was not as accomplished as I pretended to be and had to step back. I had to stop lying to myself. I had to stop focusing on material things. But what I did instead was picked up my Word and made God my partner. I let go of the world's systems and picked up Kingdom. With that came great comfort, great reassurance, and even repositioning. Yes, it was a rough time. Yes, there were sleepless nights. But those nights and that dark place helped me gain obedience and purpose. It helped me regain focus. And in the valley of my business, I learned my greatest lesson. I learned that it was never about me and that I could do nothing without God.

I realized that I do not have to know everything to feel good about myself. I just must believe in who I am and who I am called to be. Somewhere along the way, I lost my identity. I became like everyone else that I saw. I stole the ideas and characteristics of people I admired. I tried to walk in a "grace" that was not afforded to me. And when I looked in the mirror, I was confused because I did not see me. It was the face of Kim, but Kim was nowhere to be found. However, these inner adversities allowed me to become a champion – in more ways than one! And it all started with me making the decision to be who God called me to be, not the "me" that others tried to mold me into. I contribute everything to God! He told me who I was and am and was to become.

The lessons that I learned and the discipline that I was afforded have allowed me to grow and glow. From not being able to produce what I thought I wanted, to not contributing financially to the home; from not understanding my next move to seeing no increase in my business – all of these were pivotal lessons. I was clapping for others but receiving no applause. I was cheering for the names being called in major arenas, but never hearing my own. Did I cry? Absolutely! Was I angry? Undoubtedly! The tears were real and raw. But the truth of the matter is that they came from a place of deceit. You see, I tricked myself into believing that it was about me. I tricked myself into believing that I deserved the notoriety and the applause. But it was never about me. The platform was never mine to showboat and showcase "my" goodness. Instead, it was meant to be a light for others.

I have been called to help others see their purpose and live their purpose. I have been called to take the hits for those who cannot fight or speak for themselves. He has called me to help them secure themselves, as He secures me in Him. Again, this journey has nothing to do with me. It is all about others. It is all about those I am assigned to serve. And that is the difference of my before and my after.

This journey was not about my title, it was not about me and my travels, and it was not about my church home. But it was about my faith. It was about me crying out to God and allowing Him to pick up the pieces. It was all about knowing what I was created for. And this has kept me sane, especially when I felt like I was going to fall apart.

I am reminded of a book by Joel Osteen titled, "31 Promises to Speak Over Your Life." Day 22 of the declarations states, "I declare that I will live victoriously. I was created in the image of God. I have the DNA of a winner. I am wearing the crown of favor. Royal blood flows through my veins. I am the head, and never the tail. I am above and never beneath. I will live with purpose, passion, and praise; knowing that I was destined to live in victory."

This is my declaration! This is my lifeline. This is my journey. And this is what has made me the success that I am today. I revoked my membership to be popular and traded it in to join discipleship. I let go of what I thought I wanted and embraced what I needed. My favorite scripture is Matthew 6:33. It says, "But seek ye first the

Kingdom of God, and His righteousness; and all these things shall be added unto you." This has impacted my life because I deliberately get up every single day and seek HIM. The world has nothing for me, but my God shall supply every need and shows me the path I am to walk. I am grateful to serve such a consistent faithful God – especially through entrepreneurship.

BWL (Breakfast with the Lord) is effective and fruitful because we seek God's purposes.

Women and Men from across the world calculatedly depend on God for wisdom and direction. And any business or brand that fails to do so is setting themselves up for failure. I am so blessed to know that God's faithfulness to me is despite my flaws. But beyond that, I am blessed that God's Grace and Grace have brought me safe this far.

WHAT IS YOUR BURNING DESIRE? A SOULFUL PURPOSE
~Charay Dupree, Ed.D. ~

Who am I? What is my purpose? Most of us have asked ourselves these questions. The purpose of this chapter is to invite you to explore another question; What is your burning desire? In this section, you will explore who you are as an individual and what you have to offer yourself and the world at large.

Turn inward and tune into the beat of your heart, the breaths within your soul as we seek to reveal a burn that brings meaning to your existence. The desire I challenge you to conquer is one that serves the world at large while also bringing you intrinsic fulfillment. We can all agree that twitching at every flying object, shouting out our emotions after being done wrong, having that glass of wine, Pepsi cola, or indulging in a romantic encounter has its releases, but there is way more to each of us than that.

Do not just read another chapter; engage in a journey to self-discovery. Get out your notepad, tablet, or cell phones and let us take this journey together.

Getting to know you

Ideas, beliefs, principles, and thoughts are the core of all our actions. As we witness behaviors, experience events, and reenact situations, we are downloading a playlist of ideas, beliefs, and principles. As you read this chapter, write down principles, beliefs, ideas, and even experiences that guide your behavior.

How well do you know yourself? What courses did you take, or special training did you undergo to increase your self-understanding? Is understanding, who we are an automatic behavior?

As we grow and develop in our mind, body, and soul; it is important that we fully understand how parts of our bodies all work together. Just as toddlers need potty-training to void, we also must be trained to properly understand, love, and nurture ourselves. Until we master self-love, we are unable to securely administer that love and care to others.

Self-Actualization

Abraham Maslow, an American psychologist, calls mastering the self, self-actualization. Self-actualization is realizing your fullest potential. Have you mastered your fullest potential?

Less than 1% of the adult population 'self-actualize.' Due to the demands of life, the need to survive, traumatic experiences, oppressive conditions, and other social factors, many of us never fully self-actualize.

Self-Love

Perhaps the first step to self-actualization is self-love. To love yourself you must set aside time to engage in an intimate space of first acknowledging and understanding yourself. Just as you would share your likes and dislikes with others, it is important for you to know these very same things about yourself.

1. What are your traits?

2. What are your qualities?

3. What are your strengths and weaknesses?

4. What are your gifts? Abilities?

Gaining a clear understanding of who we are allows us to translate subconscious behaviors into communicated feelings. A better understanding of self leads to increased self- love, self-awareness, and improved relationships with others.

Reflecting and analyzing compliments you receive from others can enlighten you about yourself. That means constructive criticism should be invited, not avoided. Also, sitting with your own self-reflections and asking yourself the questions:

1. Why do I behave the way I do?

2. What are my values, beliefs, and goals? Why?

3. What am I missing?

Reflection and honesty can bring about increased self-love. Write down your thoughts in a journal or in your cell phone notes section. This will help you remember and hold yourself accountable.

What is your Burning Desire?

Have you ever wanted something? I mean really wanted something so bad that you could not stop thinking about it. You prayed about it. The "idea" remained in the forefront of your mind, even when you wanted to try to suppress it. It settled like a burn, a strong craving, a desire! What is your burning desire?

Let's face it, no matter who we are or what we have sought to become, most of us can admit to having desire. Whether we desired to do absolutely nothing, desired to hook up with a romantic crush, or desired to binge eat or drink a high calorie food or alcoholic beverage. This chapter is about discovering a gift, talent, ability, or trait that you innately possess.

For years I found myself frustrated with people who hurt others. I could be minding my business in the grocery store and hear the wrong tone taken and immediately go to the defense of the person being done wrong. In every job, I have always challenged processes and behaviors that undermined the good of all people. I would say to myself, just mind your business. It did not work! I often felt like something was wrong with me because I could never fit it?

Eventually, I started to attract people who craved the truthful gestures and compassionate coaching. From this place I birthed B2A Truth Coaching and Consulting. My soulful purpose was birthed out of my painful place.

Like me, you may notice a passion or extraordinary trait about yourself that is like a desire burning within. This desire may be cooking, serving, cleaning, leading, anything! Well, anything that adds respectable value to your life.

Never in a million years did I think people would pay me for my advice! But they do. I can help and support people all over the world deepen their internal strength. Now, I want to help you find your soulful purpose! What is your burning desire?

Perhaps you found your desire years ago. Maybe, you are beginning to think about your desire as you read the pages of this book. Regardless, of where you are on the journey, I challenge you to pursue that idea, product, thought, ability!

Make it: make Sense

Think about something you crave or have a strong desire to obtain. Now, consider the job you accepted, that left you fatigue and little time to spend with your family. Your burning desire is that important.

Each of us shares the same 24 hours in our day. That equals 1440 minutes. Think about how you spend those days now. Now, think about how you really want to spend those days. Write it down and create a plan. Then, do it!

If it is not pulling you up, it is weighing you down! If you look around you and you are uncomfortable with anything you see, it is your responsibility to do something about it. Follow me on all my social platforms so I can teach you how to Have Fun, cultivate a Sense of Belonging, and Use your Voice!

SILENT BREAKTHROUGH (FROM WELFARE TO WEALTH)
~Dr. Tracie Hines Lashley~

———•◦❁◦•———

"Chains of habit are too light to be felt until they are too heavy to be broken" ~Author Unknown

The weight of the world can sometimes overshadow the mind to dream BIG and go for the gusto. As time moves forward, but actions standstill, people can allow the universe to take over their movements, thoughts, and deepest desires. To be silent will overtake the inner core of our being without allowing the modest movement of lips to form the simplest whisper. Brene Brown once said, "When we deny our stories, they define us. When we own our stories, we get to write the ending." A breakthrough moment can ensure chains are broken, words are heard, and stories are released.

"He brought them out of darkness and the shadow of death and broke their chains in pieces" (NIV, Psalm 107:14)

Chains Forming Habits

I grew up in the Glenwood area of Panama City, FL, where parents worked long hours and grandparents were always around to care for children. There was no growing up privileged or with luxuries, which was not an option in the 80's. The desires of hearts may not be complete at a young age, which was the reason babysitting was my choice for income at the age of 12. My needs were always met, but my wants were frequently deferred. Caring for children was always a passion of mine, but money was the driver to afford and fulfill my wants. And even at a young age, my mother, Valinda Russell Jackson, ensured that I knew NEVER TO DEPEND ON A MAN for money. She knew that I was destined for greatness. Making my own money was exciting, which was the reason for starting a tax service at the age of 15 where I was certified to do so by the Internal Revenue Service (IRS). I was not able to legally work but had the desire to make money. By the age of 16, I decided that I would form a company named, T. Hines Enterprises. My friend and mentor, Dr. John C. Maxwell, once said words that will forever stick *"None of us can afford to have a life that is controlled by someone else..."*

Chains Building Strength

The hands on the clock and dates on the calendar continue to move. I am now 21 years old and about to become a young, single mother. I was working two jobs and doing ok but not making enough money to support a child. Soon after, I was working one great job with benefits, no place to call my own, and without reliable transportation. What can be done, or what life will we have in this situation? Fast forward to another pregnancy; a move to North Carolina, and then the embarrassment of applying for and living off welfare; a one-year-old child, 6 months pregnant, sleeping on my mother's sofa, no transportation, no job, living off welfare, and bad credit. Are you serious? This is my life now? There is no way that this situation will ever define who I was destined to be.

"Happy is the (wo)man who has broken the chains which hurt the mind." ~Ovid

Chains Breaking

Growing up, I experienced entrepreneurship firsthand. To see black-owned businesses in the "hood" was impressive and lit a spark. My maternal grandfather, the late Raymond Russell, only had a second-grade education but had a drive like no other. He made money moves across the gulf coast in construction. I was so proud to see the buildings that he helped build, and amusement park rides he designed. He built his and my grandmother's, Martha Russell, retirement home with his cousin, the late Henry Henderson, by marriage. My paternal grandmother, the late Katie Hines, was a natural-born hustler. I remember her cooking and selling plates, hosting parties and card games, and many more side hustles to make ends meet. My dad, Myron Hines, was a freelancer while working for other television stations and production companies. He would often tell me, "NEVER PUT ALL OF YOUR EGGS IN ONE BASKET." This statement stuck with me to this day. The memories of my family taking ownership of their destiny forced me to snap out of my rut and take hold of my BIG DREAMS.

Starting a business was in my genes. I finally felt that burning desire again while in my 40s. The flame that sparked this leap was working for an organization where I did not feel valued. Performing duties of my previous manager for years and not promoted after her retirement was a hard SLAP IN THE FACE and a WAKEUP CALL. I felt defeated and beat myself up bad for believing in others to do what is right. This wakeup call led me to focus on what "Tracie" needs to do for her DREAMS... I told myself to... "STOP RELYING ON OTHER PEOPLE" to value or define my worth. I had to constantly tell myself...

- "I WILL FAIL but will get back up and keep trying" ...

- "I cannot be great unless I get started" ...

- "I will leap and grow my wings on the way down" ...

- "I will become a risk-taker" ...

After finally realizing my purpose and my WHY, I started 2 companies and founded a nonprofit organization while working a full-time job and teaching for several universities. I always wanted to help other people grow and walk in their purpose. Starting my first company was just the jump start that I needed; however, resources were slim. I was able to assist clients (individuals and companies) with limited resources but always wanted more. I would always hear the saying, "You are in business FOR yourself, but NOT by yourself." I never quite knew what that saying meant until joining The John Maxwell Team. Joining this team provided so many resources to grow myself and others. This driving desire to help more people, especially women, ignited the flame to be the founder of a nonprofit organization to help women.

"A chain is no stronger than its weakest link, and life is, after all, a chain." ~ *William James*

Challenges: I faced many challenges after starting my businesses. One thing that hit me like a ton of bricks was... MONEY... I was not aware of the overall cost of starting a thriving business. One of the best parts of working while starting a business is income generated, which can be used to Purchase the tools and resources required. Working towards retirement has a new meaning for me. I am working towards retiring early and setting the foundation to live my dream fulltime. Notice that I said "live" not "work." When you do things that you love, it does not feel like work. Caring what other people thought of my dreams and actions towards moving into entrepreneurship presented a challenge. I had to remember the words of Les Brown, "someone's opinion of you does not have to become your reality."

Time is not always on my side. Being an entrepreneur is exhausting. Getting 8 hours of sleep will NOT happen while building a business. I have many restless nights, especially when the clock hits midnight, but my mind will not release thoughts and rest. One thing that helps me reduce the stress of time management is to plan my day and eliminate distractions. I had to learn the hard way that time for leisure and relaxation MUST be entered into my agenda. This tip has increased my productivity beyond measure.

"Knowing the Lord my God has set me free, by removing bondage, what would I look like walking around with self-imposed chains weighing me down? It just doesn't make sense, but people do it." ~May Fairy

Overcoming: I was able to overcome challenges. The first was to… "Get out of my head." I kept telling myself, "You can't do this" … "Who do you think you are" … "Girl, sit down somewhere and keep working for the government making six figures until you are 65 years old". I said, "Self… get your butt up and do what God has ordained for you…" I had to ask myself, "Are you calling God a liar?" God said, "You can, and you will" … God promised you the desires of your heart. God put you here for a reason… DO NOT DENY GOD to others… God placed you here for HIS will, HIS desire, and HIS purpose for YOU! STOP BEING SELFISH & WALK IN YOUR PURPOSE… So, I was able to overcome by BECOMING a woman of GOD! I acknowledged my favor and started walking in my PURPOSE. Oh yeah, remember T. Hines Enterprises? Guess what? T. Hines Enterprise, LLC became a reality in 2018.

"We are what we repeatedly do. EXCELLENCE, then, is not an act but a HABIT." ~Aristotle

Links of Legacy

I once heard the saying… "I chase PURPOSE, not paper," and it is what I am feeling today. I am walking in my PURPOSE. God did not give my purpose to anyone else; therefore, it is my duty to ensure it is fulfilled. I am on the journey to building generational wealth while helping others grow and build their legacy. You must NEVER put 100% of your energy into making someone else's dream a reality and not have any energy left to chase your own. What does this mean? It means to work your 9-5 job (or whatever your hours), then go home and work 5-9 making your dreams come true.

Stepping out on faith and allowing God to direct my path was the key to thriving in my businesses. I had to realize that doors not meant for me to walk through will be bolted. To grow myself or business, I was willing to fail, make sacrifices, take many risks, and most of all BET ON MYSELF. Nothing was ever dropped on my lap; therefore, I had to put in the work with many sleepless nights to grow a portfolio from the welfare mindset to a wealthy strategist perspective.

Cheers to living FULL and dying EMPTY!!

MEET THE COORDINATOR & AUTHORS

Dr. Anissa Short
The Coordinator of the Project

Dr. Anissa Short, also known as the Work from Home CEO, is an advocate for the home-based entrepreneur. As an entrepreneur herself, she is a leader in a top Direct Sales company, and has built an organization of clients and business partners represented in several states. Within this capacity, she has coordinated and facilitated workshops and retreats that have served to educate, encourage, and empower women in business. As a best-selling author, workshop presenter, and podcast host, she uses her platforms to offer information vital to the success of other entrepreneurs in the home-based business industry. In addition, Anissa has partnered with local community colleges, publishing and marketing companies, and training think tanks to organize, facilitate, and host events that support the success of current and aspiring entrepreneurs. She has been noted as an influencer that understands the value of building strong collaborative relationships. Prior to her entrepreneurial journey, Anissa cultivated her skill set within the industries of sales, manufacturing, banking, and over a decade of employment within the Federal Government.

Within her 20 years as an employee, she received the support and opportunities to build upon her interpersonal skills, grew to appreciate the value of building quality relationships, and establish herself as an effective communicator as she often facilitated workshops and training classes on local, statewide, and regional levels. Anissa has served on the board of two nonprofits.

She attained her BBA, MBA, and PhD in the areas of Business and Administration. She has been married to her biggest supporter, Alphonso Short since 1998, and in her spare time, enjoys reading and travel to any location with a beach and a view of the ocean.

Anita Blue

Anita Blue is a native of Fayetteville, North Carolina. After graduating from high school, she attended the University of North Carolina at Greensboro where she received her bachelor's degree in English Education. Shortly after graduating from college, she began teaching in the Cumberland County School system.

Anita has always had a passion for teaching and that passion goes beyond the four walls of a classroom. She has taught in various settings to include her church and at after school and summer tutoring facilities. Spending quality time with her family is what makes life worthwhile for Anita.

She is married to an extraordinary husband and they have three incredible children. She is a pastor alongside her husband at Clinton International Church in Clinton, NC. She is also a licensed realtor in the state of North Carolina. Anita's favorite motivational quote is one she created, "When you have an excellent attitude, excellent actions are inevitable."

Monchaily Hendricks

Monchaily Hendricks is a Fayetteville native born and raised in the golden era of break dancing, funk, and big hair. As a military brat, she knows the value of hard work and gives her all into any project she undertakes, even if it means extra cups of coffee.

As an entrepreneur, Monchaily (aka Molly) is known as a savvy, administrative organizer who catapults business owners and families into success through creative services with her company, Xelbooks. Whether its organization, resume, web design or even home improvement, she gives creativity a run for its money. However, business is just the tip of the iceberg for Monchaily.

She currently holds a BBA from Keiser University. In addition, she is currently obtaining two Comptia certifications, a Microsoft certification, and a Project management certification. When not working, she enjoys spending time with her two AMAZING boys (Zion and Micah), as well as listening to music and doing Zumba. Be sure to check out her buffet of at www dot x e l books .com.

Driven, talented, creative, she can fit into all those boxes, but the best way to summarize her is to say that she is a woman of God.

Peggy Green

Peggy Green is originally from Washington County, in Glen Allan, Mississippi, but grew up in another small town in Issaquena County, Mayersville, Mississippi. She is the oldest of 5 girls and 3rd oldest of 9 children. Peggy was adamant reader. She would sit under her big tree at home and read for hours, finishing novels in days.

She graduated from South Delta High School in Rolling Fork, Mississippi and she attended Hinds Community College, majoring in Physical Education because of her love for fitness & health. She has been actively building a business in the Direct Sales Industry for 13 years and a Retail Banker.

Peggy is a free spirit of the sort, she never got entangled into others' opinions of her. Her journey is simply that Hers; She is now pursuing other areas of entrepreneur business. It will lead others to a healthier lifestyle flow as well.

Look for her name is in the Health Industry soon!

La Tondra C. Lewis

Reverend LaTondra C. Lewis hails from the state of Tennessee and is the sole proprietor of TAKE A PEW Holistic Health Lounge.

In addition to teaching pre-kindergarten within the local school district, LaTondra heeded to another vocation which was the call to ministry. She has served in her local church for many years and then entered the pastorate at Seeds of Life Church, a ministry that spans over twenty-seven years.

LaTondra holds a B.A. degree in Social Work from LeMoyne-Owen College. As a social worker, she held various positions in the areas of mental health, children, and youth services (residential) housing development and foster care. As a two-time bilateral breast cancer survivor, she recently celebrated twenty-two years of being cancer free. This accomplishment has afforded a life of normalcy and the opportunity to be a part of some the greatest organizations,

Les Gemmes, Inc., Delta Sigma Theta Sorority, Inc., and Charmettes, Inc.

LaTondra's favorite quote is the scripture she lives by and that is 3 John 1:2: *Beloved, I wish above all things that thou mayest prosper and be in health, even as thy soul prospereth.*

JurLonna Walker

JurLonna Walker Hermon is a native of Fayetteville, North Carolina and currently resides in North Carolina and St. Thomas, U.S. Virgin Islands with her husband. She is known as a Purpose Strategist, a cheerleader for Christians to live their authentic life. As an author, she released her first book in 2017, "Follow Your Breadcrumbs" that helped individuals to discover their purpose. She shares her journey of how staying connected with God reveals your purpose. As an entrepreneur, she assists Kingdom Leaders by helping them to share their message with the world through book publishing. She also partners with her husband with their boat charter management company in St. Thomas, Virgin Islands.

Prior to her business endeavors, JurLonna worked in the fields of Customer Service, Economic Development, and approximately ten years within Higher Education. While employed within each sector, she served as a leader in mentoring and training employees whether locally, state-wide, or regionally.

In addition to her professional endeavors, her educational background includes bachelor's in psychology and master's in Business and Administration with a concentration in Human Resources Management.

JurLonna enjoys traveling and hanging out with family and friends.

Ebony M. Walker

If you ever wanted to know what resilience looks like, the name and the person of Ebony M. Walker would be exemplary. Wife, Mother, Daughter, Sister, Entrepreneur, Pastor, Author, Mentor, Friend. These are just a few of the many hats that she wears. Born and raised in Moore County, North Carolina, this Eastwood (Pinehurst) native has defeated many odds and has survived things that are unspeakable. From molestation to abandonment, from drug infested environments to depression - she should have been another negative statistic. But God had another plan for her.

Earning a degree in Criminal Justice, she worked in the Legal System as a Paralegal and a Background Investigator for a short time. Music, writing, and motivational speaking have always been passions of hers. She is the Owner of Walk UpWrite, which provides copywriting, ghostwriting, and more! Her clientele list is vast, as she has served an array of people with various writing projects. From Politicians to Clergymen, from Activists to Multi-Million Dollar Entertainers, from Teachers to Mothers and Fathers, from CEOs to College Students - she shares her gift with people from all walks of life.

She was ordained as a Pastor in 2015, selected as a "Think Smart 40 Under 40" Honoree, is a North Carolina Notary, and has served as the North Carolina Chapter Leader for JNG (Jus' Networking Girlz) for over 5 years. This is an international female entrepreneur networking group that helps women across the globe to build their audience and their bank accounts, providing support and resources to one another. In March of 2019, "Beauty in the Pulpit" was released. This is her 1st co-authored project, with several other ministerial leading ladies. It discusses the "behind the scenes" detriment that many women have faced in ministry but were too ashamed to disclose.

Featured on ABC, Fox News, CBS, Boston Herald, Telemundo, Majority Greek Magazine, Kueez Entertainment, Atlanta Live, and many other platforms, she is focused on reaching the masses via marketplace ministry. A motivational speaker and a woman of prayer, Ebony is one who whole heartedly relies on the grace of God to function and complete any assignment given to her.

She currently resides in Fayetteville, NC with her husband, Apostle John Walker. Collectively, they have 4 children, 7 grandchildren, and 1 special Goddaughter.

Latoya Harrington

Award Winning, Fashion Designer and Pastor **Latoya Harrington** is the wife of Benjamin Harrington and mother of three boys Jonquil Jr., Jalyn, and Jaden Walker. She was born and raised in Concord, North Carolina, and is the owner and lead seamstress of Sew Fab & Company.

Latoya is the writer and stage director of the I AM FAB Dramatic Runway Show. She has recently launched her non-profit organization, Embracing Me, helping young women and girls to live in their full potential. In 2018, she won Fashion Designer of the year for ACHI Magazine.

Latoya serves in ministry as an Elder and is passionate about sharing Christ with others. She exemplifies her ministry and gifts through her clothing line. Sewing and helping women to feel confident is great part of her "ministry meets fashion".

Her business and mentorship have provided many opportunities for her to serve and give back to the community.

AnneMarie Ziegler

AnneMarie Ziegler has always enjoyed coloring outside the lines, thinking outside the box, and stepping across lines drawn in the sand. A Cumberland County native of 8 generations she is the owner and operator of the only woman owned publishing company in the county.

What began as one local variety magazine almost seven years ago now includes the only Latino publication in the county, as well as various events throughout the year providing opportunities for businesses and nonprofits.

Married to Paul for 14 years, mother to four children and grandmother to six, AnneMarie proudly proclaims to be a workaholic and #ladyboss.

A nice glass of wine, a good book, spending time with family, and long walks on the beach are a few of her favorite pleasures…when not working passionately for the local community and businesses, or looking for a new "project" to take on!

Dr. J. Michelle Vann

Michelle Vann, DCC is the CEO and Founder of Sistahs Can We Talk. She serves the world as a Confidence Coach through Vanntastic Solutions, as well as a Motivational Speaker and Author. She is the wife of Pastor Dr. William G Vann. They have been married for 30 years and they are the proud parents of Brandon and Brianna both of whom are building their own paths within the community.

Michelle served in the Wichita Public Schools for 20 years, before moving to Friends University to work in the office of Admissions as the Dual Credit Coordinator. She has a Bachelor of Arts in Elementary Education, a master's in liberal studies, and Doctorate in Christian Counseling as well as her ministerial licensure from Victorious Life Bible College.

Vann has served in ministry with her husband for 26 years in various capacities. She is very involved in church, and many community organizations that promote the uplifting of women and health. Finally, she is the author of two books Help Along the Journey and Stop the Merry-go-round I want to get off.

She is presently working with two anthology projects to launch in the fall.

Michelle believes that we must pull the lessons out every situation and when we do we can truly walk in our calling.

Dr. Belinda J. Wilkerson

Dr. Belinda J. Wilkerson, the founder and principal counselor of Steps to the Future, LLC, a college and career counseling practice, serves high school students and young adults transitioning to postsecondary education and/or a career. A lifelong educator, Dr. Wilkerson held positions as a Social Studies teacher, a professional school counselor, counselor educator and counselor- in-residence. In the counselor-in-residence position, she developed statewide guidance and career curriculum, created professional development opportunities for professional school counselors and mentored educators new to the school counseling profession.

She earned a B.A in Secondary Education/History and a M.Ed. in Counselor Education from Rhode Island College, in addition to an Eddy in Educational Leadership from Johnson & Wales University. In 2004, the Rhode School Counselor Association (RISCA) honored her as the Rhode Island School Counselor of the Year, an award voted on by her peers. The American School

Counselor Association (ASCA) recognized her work as the Counselor- in-Residence at Providence College with their Counseling Director/Coordinator of the Year award in 2007. Additionally, the Rhode Island School Counselor Association awarded Dr. Wilkerson a Lifetime

Achievement award in 2010.

Throughout her career, Dr. Wilkerson mentored students at every level. As a middle school teacher, she developed a weekend program for a small group of seventh graders consisting of outings to various events in the state and discussing issues of importance to the group. As a high school teacher and school counselor, she advised the Multicultural Club, an afterschool program dedicated to service in the community such as volunteering at a soup kitchen and visiting senior centers several times a year.

Active in the Cumberland County community, Dr. Wilkerson serves as the Chair of the Cumberland County Library Board of Trustees. As a trustee, she attends monthly trustee meetings, represents the library's interests at Cumberland County Commissioners' meetings and encourages literacy through public speaking engagements and social media. Entering her sixth year, Dr. Wilkerson volunteers weekly with the Chill ax Teen Program at East Regional Public Library where she engages middle and high school students in conversations and activities about their postsecondary options and career choices. As a member of the Board of Directors for the Independent Educational Consultants

Association (IECA), Belinda mentors new IECs and previously served on the Education & Training Committee. Elected for a second term of office, Dr. Wilkerson is the 2019-2021 Vice President of Ethics and Business Practices for IECA.

Volunteering as an usher with the Cape Fear Regional Theatre allows her to satisfy her love for theater while giving back to her community. She enjoys time with her husband and their fur family, two dogs and two cats, in addition to visiting their sons and other family, reading extensively, and traveling. To contact her: doctorb@steps2thefuture.com

CHERYL S. (CHERIE) HALL

Cherie's early life, which began in Memphis, TN, was rooted and grounded in church and God. She grew up as Pastor's Kid (PK), and was very active in her church choir, as well as administrative tasks for the church office. She often says that God gave her three gifts: Singing, Typing and Playing the Tambourine!

She also began her love for acting with her local church but did not really pursue it further until about 10 years ago. Cherie continues to be active in her current church choir, sings with the Praise Team, and is a member of several groups, including one that travels once a year overseas during the holiday season.

In addition to her three gifts, Cherie also has a love for travel, and became a Travel Advisor in January 2016. This love, given by her Mom, has been enhanced through her business. In fact, she has several business ventures that now showcase the sum parts of her "world", Cherie's World.

You can learn more by visiting her website <u>at</u> <u>www.cheriesworld.com.</u> Cherie is married to Leo Hall, and has two adult children, Lee, and Jared. She and Leo have been married for almost 29 years.

Kim Meyers

Preacher, Teacher, and Reacher! Minister **Kim Meyers**, born April 13, 1968 was raised in Bronx, New York by a true example – a distinguished and phenomenal woman named Gracie Green and she still relishes in being a daddy's girl to her father, Edward Green. Having accepted Christ at only 8 years old, Kim embraced her calling to preach the Word of God and became a licensed Minister in 2017. She has a Bachelor of Science Degree in Divinity, and Spiritual Counseling from Liberty University. Kim served as an Associate Minister at Mt. Zion Baptist Church in Triangle, Virginia under the leadership of Rev. Dr. Alfred Jones Jr.

Kim began her professional business in Direct Sales in 2001. Her tenacity and drive have propelled her to flourish expeditiously, rising to the top 2% of the company as a Sales Director. During her 20-year career, she has earned countless medals of achievements, numerous awards nominated by her peers, free cars as well as free vacations. She has also served as a Lead Liaison within countless Prestigious Programs in the Direct Sales arena.

In 2017, Kim launched a women's empowerment movement LLC called "I AM ENOUGH." This global organization teaches women how to walk unapologetically in their purpose and passion. She is the Founder and Visionary Leader of "Breakfast with the Lord" better known as BWL, a global Morning Prayer call. BWL is an amazing platform for the everyday woman and man to enhance their relationship with God, to start their day off with motivation, inspiration, empowerment, encouragement, and purpose.

Kim serves in an array of endeavors such as Motivational Speaker, Empowerment Leader, Spiritual Counseling, Event Planner (local and destination weddings, birthday party, graduation party, etc.), volunteering in nursing homes, women's shelters, homeless shelters, and feeding the homeless. Kim even became a Certified Nursing Assistant (CNA), and Licensed Practical Nurse (LPN) to aid her ailing mother-in-love during a prolonged illness.

Kim's favorite scriptures that have imparted the strength to prevail are Philippians 4:13 "I can do all things through Christ who strengthens me", and Matthew 6:33 "But seek ye first the kingdom of God and His righteousness, and all these things shall be added to you."

Kim has been married to her soul mate, Keith K. Meyers, CPA for 24 years, describing him as "the wind beneath her wings". Currently living in Oregon, they have two adult children, Jamar and Shanelle.

Charay S. Dupree, Ed.D.

Dr. Charay Dupree, affectionately known as Dr. Charay, is an educator, community leader, and truth coach. Charay has sought to empower the lives of oppressed and hopeless persons through education, counseling, ministry, and leadership for more than 15 years. She serves as a ghost writer for upcoming authors, a mentor and coach to individuals seeking deeper internal strength, and a mother to four young men (D'Quantez (18), Jayden (15), Christian (8), and Donald (5) At the early age of 12, Charay's passion and love for teaching was birthed as a Sunday school teacher in her local congregation. Professionally, she embraced a career as a teacher, school counselor, and principal.

Dr. Charay has earned a Bachelor's in Education, Masters in School Administration and Counseling, and a Doctor of Educational Leadership. As a leader in her profession and community Charay is the author of three books: *Bring it to an A, Academic Group Manual (2014), A Dose of Truth (2015),* and *A Dose of Truth Platinum (2019).*

Understanding the need for diversity and inclusion of marginalized persons in positions of power and influence, Charay established B2A Truth Coaching and Consulting, an engagement and advising firm that assist business owners and leaders with strategic planning, content development, and empowerment training.

Charay's civic engagement includes an appointed, full-term membership to the Fayetteville-Cumberland Board of Appeals and a 2019 Climate Reality Leader certification under the leadership of former Vice President Al Gore (with the support of former NAACP president Dr. William Barber and the Poor People's campaign).

Pastor Charay leads from the scripture I Peter 3:17 & 18, for it is better, if the will of God be so, that ye suffer for well doing, than for evil doing. For Christ also hath once suffered for the sins, the just for the unjust, that he might bring us to God, being put to death in the flesh, but quickened by the spirit. Thereby, her favorite scripture is I John 3:18, My little children, let us not love in word, neither in tongue; but in deed and truth.

Charay finds great satisfaction in her work as a minister and advocate for social justice. But grow in grace, and in the knowledge of our Lord and Savior Jesus Christ. To him be glory both now and forever, Amen (2 Peter 3:18).

Dr. Tracie Hines Lashley

Tracie Lashley, known as The LeadHERz Architect, is dedicated to helping female bosses harmonize the art and science of leadership and reach the pinnacle (respect) level while strategizing team effectiveness and productivity. In addition to this, her non-profit, Boss'd UP LeadHERz, Inc., serves to create a united force of women business owners and leaders, while developing young girls to govern the world and relieve the QUEEN BEE SYNDROME!

With a doctoral degree in management specializing in organizational leadership, Tracie also holds two MBA degrees, one in Human Resource Management and the other in Technology Management, a BS degree in Database Technology and an Administrative Degree in business administration. She is currently working on a MS degree in performance improvement.

Tracie is a college professor for several universities and a supervisor for a federal government agency. She is also the CEO of THE Leaders Innovative Growth Solutions and an Executive Director of The John Maxwell Team.

In 2020, Tracie co-authored several books, including "The NEW Female Leader" and one with Dr. Cheryl Wood "Courageous Enough to Launch. When she is not working and committing herself to continued educational endeavors, she loves to sing, dance, write (especially poetry) listen to a variety of music, forex trading, investing, and helping others grow.

Her favorite quote regarding Leadership is by Jim Rohn, "The challenge of leadership is to be strong, but not rude; be kind, but not weak; be bold, but not bully; be thoughtful, but not lazy; be humble, but not timid; be proud, but not arrogant; have humor, but without folly."